THE BIG FAT

MIDDLE SCHOOL

ENGLISH LANGUAGE ARTS WORKBOOK

WORKMAN PUBLISHING
NEW YORK

Workman Kids
Workman Publishing
Hachette Book Group, Inc.
1290 Avenue of the Americas
New York, NY 10104
workman.com

Workman Kids is an imprint of Workman Publishing, a division of Hachette Book Group, Inc. BRAIN QUEST, BIG FAT NOTE-BOOK, and the Workman name and logo are registered trademarks of Hachette Book Group, Inc.

Writer: Kelly Scardina
Contributing Writer: Keisha Rembert
Designer: Abby Dening
Art Direction: Keirsten Geise
Illustrator: Niallycat

The publisher is not responsible for websites (or their content) that are not owned by the publisher.

Workman books may be purchased in bulk for business, educational, or promotional use. For information, please contact your local bookseller or the Hachette Book Group Special Markets Department at special.markets@hbgusa.com.

ISBN: 978-1-5235-2371-9

First Edition September 2024

Distributed in Europe by Hachette Livre, 58 rue Jean Bleuzen, 92 178 Vanves Cedex, France.
Distributed in the United Kingdom by Hachette UK Ltd., Carmelite House,
50 Victoria Embankment, London EC4Y 0DZ.

Printed in Shenzhen, China (IMSF) 02/25 on responsibly sourced paper.

10 9 8 7 6 5 4 3 2

WELCOME TO YOUR BIG FAT WORKBOOK.

This workbook is designed to support you as you work your way through *Everything You Need to Ace English Language Arts in One Big Fat Notebook* or through your middle school English class. Consider the *Notebook* your main sourcebook and this *Workbook* extra practice.

Each chapter in this workbook corresponds with a chapter in the *Notebook*. They will have the same name! *Workbook* chapters begin with a brief recap of the key concepts, followed by a series of extra practice activities for you to complete—from vocabulary review to analyzing poems to writing exercises.

In the back of the book there is an in-depth answer key you can use to check your work. It includes explanations to explain concepts you might be struggling with. And for questions that don't have one right answer, it includes sample answers and a simple rubric you can use to check your own work.

Whether you're reviewing for a test or need to strengthen your writing skills, look no further than this companion workbook. You'll encounter the same fun, easy-to-understand approach to ELA that you love in *Everything You Need to Ace English Language Arts in One Big Fat Notebook*.

Together you'll have everything you need to ACE that English class!

CONTENTS

UNIT 1: GRAMMAR 1

1. Sentences **2**
2. Pronouns **22**
3. Active and Passive Voice **39**
4. Verbs and Mood **55**
5. Verbals **66**
6. Defining from Context **82**
7. Affixes and Roots **96**
8. Reference Materials **112**

UNIT 2: LANGUAGE 131

9. Figurative Language **132**
10. Word Choice **150**
11. Tone **166**
12. Textual Analysis **178**

UNIT 3: WRITING 197

13. Writing Narratives **198**
14. The Writing Process **218**
15. Research for Writing **236**
16. Media Literacy **252**
17. Expository Writing **270**
18. Writing Arguments **290**

ANSWER KEY 313

Unit 1

GRAMMAR

Grammar is the structure of a language—not what words mean, but the rules that explain how they can work together to build sentences, paragraphs, and more!

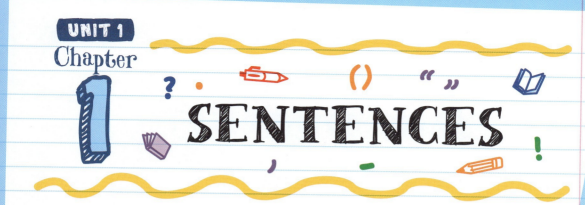

UNIT 1
Chapter 1
SENTENCES

SENTENCES are formed by words, phrases, and clauses.

A **PHRASE** is a group of words that acts as a single part of speech. A phrase can't be a complete sentence because it is always missing either a subject or a verb.

Examples:

noun phrase
I caught three wriggly fish.

The music was much louder on the dance floor.
← *adjective phrase*

THINK:
If your friend says, "the polka-dot tie," you might be confused and ask, "Well, what about the polka-dot tie?" There's no verb in that statement! It's a phrase.

SUBJECT
You can identify the subject of a sentence by asking yourself: *Who or what is the sentence about?* OR *Who or what is performing the action?*

Examples:
subject
The acrobat performed several tricks on the tightrope.

The ringmaster and clown opened the circus with enthusiasm.
← *subjects* →

PARTS OF SPEECH

NOUN: a word that identifies or names

Think: a person, place, thing, feeling, or idea

ADJECTIVE: a word that **MODIFIES** or describes a noun

Think: color, size, shape, texture, type, or sound

VERB: a word that expresses action or a state of being

Think: action or state of existence

> **MODIFY**
> to describe or provide more information about a word, phrase, or clause

ADVERB: a word that modifies a verb, adjective, or another adverb

Think: How? When? Where? How often? In what way?

PREPOSITION: a word or group of words that expresses relationship

Think: direction, time, place, or location

A **CLAUSE** is a group of words that always includes a subject and a verb.

Example:

▶ you dyed your hair pink

subject   verb

There are two types of clauses:

An **INDEPENDENT CLAUSE** can stand alone as a complete sentence.

Example:

We roasted s'mores.

This is a complete idea!

A **DEPENDENT CLAUSE** can't stand alone as a complete sentence. It depends on help from other words or phrases to express a complete idea.

Example:

dependent clause

When the campfire was ready, we roasted s'mores.

help!

There are three types of dependent clauses:

1. **NOUN CLAUSE**: a dependent clause that acts like a noun

A DEPENDENT CLAUSE NEVER ACTS LIKE A VERB.

2. **ADJECTIVE CLAUSE**: a dependent clause that acts like an adjective

3. **ADVERB CLAUSE**: a dependent clause that acts like an adverb

A **SENTENCE** is a group of **words**, **clauses**, and **phrases** that expresses a complete idea. A sentence only needs a subject and a verb, but adding phrases and clauses makes it more complex.

Examples:

<u>They</u> <u>ate</u>.
subject — verb

<u>They</u> <u>ate</u> <u>delicious pizza</u> <u>all day long!</u>
subject — verb — phrase — dependent clause

There are four types of sentences:

A **SIMPLE SENTENCE** has one independent clause.

▶ I love pizza.

A **COMPOUND SENTENCE** has two or more independent clauses.

▶ <u>I love pizza</u> because <u>it is delicious</u>.
independent clause 1 — independent clause 2

A **COMPLEX SENTENCE** has one independent clause and one or more dependent clauses.

▶ <u>Because Oscar loves pizza</u>, <u>he got a job at a pizza parlor.</u>
dependent clause — independent clause

A **COMPOUND COMPLEX SENTENCE** has at least two independent clauses and at least one dependent clause.

dependent clause   independent clause 1

▶ Because Oscar loves pizza, he got a job at a pizza parlor, and he is very happy!

independent clause 2

CONJUNCTIONS are words that link words, phrases, or clauses together in a sentence.

COORDINATING CONJUNCTIONS connect independent clauses. They are always placed between the clauses.

COORDINATING CONJUNCTIONS:
for, and, nor, but, or, yet, so, since

Example:

coordinating conjunction

The sun is out, (so) I am using lots of sunscreen!

independent clause 1

independent clause 2

SUBORDINATING CONJUNCTIONS connect independent clauses to dependent clauses.

SUBORDINATING CONJUNCTIONS:
after, as, because, before, even though, if, since, until, whenever, whether

Example:

We keep our snow boots in the basement (until) winter comes.

independent clause

subordinating conjunction

dependent clause

Common Sentence Mistakes

A **MISPLACED MODIFIER** is a word, phrase, or clause that's in the wrong place, so it's not clear what the word is describing.

Example:

~~misplaced modifier~~

✗ Topped with whipped cream and a cherry, Miguel couldn't resist the hot fudge sundae.

THINK:
Was Miguel topped with whipped cream and a cherry? No! The sundae was!

✓ Miguel couldn't resist the hot fudge sundae topped with whipped cream and a cherry.

↖ modifier makes sense!

<mark>TO FIX:</mark> Bring the modifier closer to what it modifies.

A **DANGLING MODIFIER** is a word, phrase, or clause that describes something that doesn't exist in the sentence.

Example:

dangling modifier

✗ Famished, the tray of hot dogs was gobbled up.

THINK:
Who gobbled up all the hot dogs? Whoever was famished isn't mentioned in the sentence.

modifier   the missing subject!

✓ Famished, the hockey players gobbled up the tray of hot dogs.

<mark>TO FIX:</mark> Add the missing subject!

EXERCISE 1

Match each term to the correct definition.

1. Conjunction _____

2. Phrase _____

3. Clause _____

4. Verb _____

5. Independent clause _____

6. Dependent clause _____

7. Preposition _____

8. Misplaced modifier _____

A. A word that expresses a relationship to direction, location, or time

B. A group of words that includes at least a subject and a verb

C. A clause that can stand alone as a complete sentence

D. A group of words that acts as a single part of speech

E. A word that links words, phrases, and clauses in a sentence

F. A descriptive word, phrase, or clause in the wrong place

G. A word that describes an action or state of being

H. A clause that can't stand alone as a complete sentence

EXERCISE 2

What part of speech is the teal word? Write it on the line.

↳ noun, verb, adverb, adjective, preposition

1. She found the remote under the couch cushion. _____

2. Valerie ran for class president. _____

3. The film won several awards. _____

4. This is where I grew up. _____

5. Marcia thought she did well at tryouts. _____

6. Darkness settled over the campsite. _____

7. Luke's cologne lingered in the hall. _____

8. Clyde met his coach on the field. _____

9. They climbed the bleachers. _____

10. The shoes were too expensive. _____

EXERCISE 3

For each sentence, decide if the teal words form a **PHRASE** or a **CLAUSE**.

Clauses always have a subject and a verb!

1. They went to the zoo with their classmates. Phrase Clause

2. You can't watch the R-rated movie unless you have permission. Phrase Clause

3. Practicing is the only way you can learn guitar. Phrase Clause

4. Hunter is playing along even though they are confused. Phrase Clause

5. The skate park was open even though it was raining. Phrase Clause

6. Spencer was hiding in the game room. Phrase Clause

7. Xiu skied while Nick snowboarded. Phrase Clause

8. Before the inning was over, it began to rain. Phrase Clause

9. Help, I'm stuck in the middle! Phrase Clause

10. Abhinav sipped a lassi in the sunshine. Phrase Clause

EXERCISE 4

Find a phrase and a clause in each sentence.
Circle the (CLAUSE.) Underline the **PHRASE**.

Psst! If you're stuck, look for a verb. Clauses will always have a verb!

1. After the storm, the campers continued their hike.

2. The teacher lectured the pranksters about their unruly behavior.

3. The students played foursquare on the blacktop.

4. In the forest, there was little light.

5. The dirt bike skidded across the gravel.

6. Throughout the performance, the child fidgeted.

7. The chocolate ice cream dripped on her white vest.

8. There is a huge sale on LeBron sneakers!

9. The fruit bat slept peacefully until sunset.

10. Tricia found her Earth Science classroom on the second floor.

BONUS QUESTION!
How many sentences have an independent clause? _____

EXERCISE 5

Do the teal words form a **DEPENDENT CLAUSE** or an **INDEPENDENT CLAUSE?** Write your answer on the line.

1. As Devon read the chapter, she annotated carefully. _____

2. They couldn't go to the fair because of the thunderstorm. _____

3. The seagull flew off before the children could catch it. _____

4. If you don't pass the final exam, you must retake the course. _____

5. Fans screamed wildly when the band started to play. _____

6. Before he hit the court, Juan tied his sneakers tightly.   _____

7. The fortune teller closed her eyes before she read the cards.   _____

8. When they visited the animal shelter, the family adopted a golden terrier.   _____

9. In the old tool shed, Abuelo found his binoculars.   _____

10. Our class turtle fell asleep under the heat lamp.   _____

Use a coordinating conjunction from the word bank to turn each set of simple sentences into one compound sentence. Use each coordinating conjunction once.

> for   and   nor   but   or
> yet   so   since

1. The pizza finally arrived. They got our order wrong!

2. I can't swim well. I stay in the shallow end.

3. I went home. The rain wouldn't let up.

Psst! You can reword sentences if you need to!

4. She didn't try the shrimp. She also didn't try the oysters.

5. The Ferris wheel was stuck. The brave children were not afraid.

6. Frank bought a hot dog. Matilda bought a vanilla shake.

7. We can go to the concert. We can stay home.

8. Richie's mother was shocked. Richie had dyed his hair blue.

EXERCISE 7

Use coordinating conjunctions to create six complex sentences from the clauses below.

REMEMBER:
A complex sentence has one independent clause and at least one dependent clause.

INDEPENDENT CLAUSES:
her cheeks flushed
she started to believe in ghosts
I love to eat chocolate
I will go to the party with you
we brought binoculars
we drove to the airport safely

DEPENDENT CLAUSES:
even in the snow
if you wake me up
despite my allergy
because we are birdwatching
when she fell off the chair
as she got older

1.

2.

3.

4.

5.

6.

Circle the subordinating conjunction in each sentence.

EXERCISE 8

Write an example of each sentence type.

1. Simple sentence:

2. Complex sentence:

3. Compound sentence:

4. Compound complex sentence:

EXERCISE 9

Underline the **MISPLACED MODIFIER** or circle the **DANGLING MODIFIER** in each sentence. Then rewrite the sentence to fix it.

1. Fumbling in her backpack, the wallet was not found.

2. Melting in the sun made the table sticky.

3. The waiter served a steak to the guest that was too rare.

4. Crying in the emergency room, the nurse stitched Keith's wound.

5. The tourist bought a crepe from the friendly vendor covered in powdered sugar.

6. Expecting a meteor shower, the telescope was positioned correctly.

7. Driving to the party, the cake tilted dangerously in the passenger seat.

8. Kristina saw a black cat on her way to the Halloween party.

9. My parents bought a parrot for my sister with big red feathers.

10. Elaine walked the poodle wearing her prom dress.

EXERCISE 10

Find eight mistakes in the paragraph below. Then rewrite the paragraph so it's correct.

On the first day of summer vacation. I was excited to relax and unwind at the beach with my family. Ate breakfast quickly and dashed to the car. Ready to go! Riding along in the back seat, the beach suddenly came into view. I couldn't wait to sink my toes into the sand. We carried all the beach gear to our spot, I was finally able to relax. I closed my eyes and listened as seagulls squawked overhead. Crashing on the shore, I could hear the waves. The sun's rays felt warm on my skin. A gentle breeze blew since ruffled my hair. Next to me, my brother and dad planned their sandcastle. We arrived at the beach early the sandcastle could be gigantic!

Mistakes will include misplaced and dangling modifiers, conjunction errors, and incomplete sentences.

PRONOUNS

A **PRONOUN** is a word that takes the place of a noun.

Example:

"It" takes the place of "candy bar."

Dillon's candy bar melted when he left it in the sun.

"He" takes the place of "Dillon."

SUBJECTIVE PRONOUNS take the place of the subject of a sentence.

Examples:

You are honest.

What is going on?

> **SUBJECTIVE PRONOUNS:**
>
> I, you, he, she, ze, it, we, they, what, who

OBJECTIVE PRONOUNS take the place of the **OBJECT** of a sentence.

Examples:

The travel plans fell on Marissa because **she** is responsible.

This chair is heavy. The painters needed to move **it** .

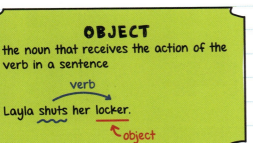

OBJECT

the noun that receives the action of the verb in a sentence

verb

Layla shuts her locker.

object

POSSESSIVE PRONOUNS show who something belongs to.

Examples:

Are the purple ski boots **mine** or **yours** ?

Bryan lost **his** antique locket.

YOURS or YOURS?

The pronoun "yours" can be **SINGULAR** or **PLURAL**. It can be used to show one person owns something or many people share ownership.

Example:

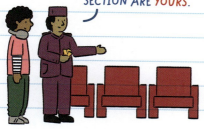

THE SEATS IN THIS SECTION ARE YOURS.

THE SEATS IN THIS SECTION ARE YOURS.

Singular Pronouns

I, me, my, myself, himself, herself, themself, you, your, it, anyone, everyone, anybody, nobody, either, neither, each, someone, somebody

Singular or Plural Pronouns

they, them, all, more, most, none, some, yours

Plural Pronouns

we, us, ourselves, yourselves, themselves, both, few, several, many

REFLEXIVE PRONOUNS refer to a noun or pronoun used earlier in a sentence. They always end in -self or -selves.

Examples:

Jessamyn blamed herself .

After practice, I drew
myself a hot bath.

INDEFINITE PRONOUNS refer to people, places, or things that are not specific or exact.

INDEFINITE PRONOUNS:
everyone, nobody,
several, everywhere,
nowhere

Examples:

Hurry, everyone is already at the party!

Nobody understands this grammar
lesson.

THINK:
Pronouns help us be less repetitive.
Instead of saying the name of
something or someone over and over
and over, you can use a pronoun!

Pronoun Problems

An **INAPPROPRIATE SHIFT** occurs when a noun is replaced by the wrong type of pronoun. There are two types to avoid:

WRONG NUMBER is when a singular pronoun replaces a plural noun or when a plural pronoun replaces a singular noun.

singular

✗ When I sat by the pool, we got splashed.

plural

WRONG CASE is when an objective pronoun is used to replace a subject, or a subjective pronoun is used to replace an object.

✗ Me play the drums.

objective pronoun replacing the subject

TO FIX: Replace the incorrect pronoun with a correct pronoun.

plural

✓ When we sat by the pool, we got splashed.

plural

✓ I play the drums.

subjective pronoun replacing the subject

A **COMPOUND PRONOUN** is a combination of nouns and pronouns that act as the subject or object of a sentence.

Examples:
▶ Me and you
▶ Jamal and I
▶ She and Kim

People often pair the wrong pronouns. To avoid that mistake, remember two important rules:

1. CORRECT ORDER: All pronouns except "I" go before the noun. "I" always comes after the noun.

✗ Jax and she saw the movie.   ✓ She and Jax saw the movie.

✗ I and Jax were at the movie.   ✓ Jax and I were at the movie.

2. CORRECT CASE: The pronoun case needs to match the sentence.

incorrect case

✗ (Him) and Felix ate forty-one hot dogs.

correct case

✓ (He) and Felix ate forty-one hot dogs.

THINK:
If you aren't sure which pronouns to use in a compound pronoun, use each in its own sentence.

should be "He"

✗ Him ate forty-one hot dogs.   ✓ Felix ate forty-one hot dogs.

EXERCISE 1

Circle all the PRONOUNS in the passage below.

Last week, I finally got a dog! Convincing my parents was not an easy task. It took strong persuasive skills. My mother is allergic to animals. When she is near them, she sneezes and her eyes get itchy. Sometimes she even breaks out in hives! My father, on the other hand, was worried a dog would scratch up the hardwood floors or ruin his favorite sneakers. He also argued that owning a dog is a large responsibility. "Are you going to walk it every day?" he asked. "Who is going to pick up the poop? I myself will absolutely not!"

Nobody thought I had a chance, but I came up with a clever plan. For weeks, I helped with lots of chores to show my parents I am responsible. I hid pictures of adorable Goldendoodle puppies everywhere, even under their pillows! Who could resist those soft brown eyes, tiny paws, and fluffy tails? To everyone's surprise, my parents relented. Overjoyed, I named our new dog Viking. She is the cutest dog in the whole world! We love her very much.

1. What subjective pronouns are used?

2. Find a reflexive pronoun:

3. Find a possessive pronoun:

4. Find an indefinite pronoun:

EXERCISE 2

Circle the (SUBJECT) and underline the **OBJECT** in each sentence.

1. Jacob cut the grass.

2. The lifeguard rescued the drowning swimmer.

3. For dessert, I picked a king-size candy bar.

4. Phineas ate the cheeseburger, even though it was cold.

5. The tornado destroyed the home in five seconds flat.

6. My teacher took attendance.

7. The van pulled into the parking lot.

8. She decorated the cupcakes with purple icing.

9. The chef grilled the lamb chops.

10. We could not connect to the internet.

EXERCISE 3

Circle the (PRONOUNS) in each sentence. State if the pronoun is **SUBJECTIVE** or **OBJECTIVE** by writing an **S** or an **O** above it.

Psst! Some pronouns can be both subjective and objective. Pay attention to how each pronoun is used in the sentence.

1. I bought some new ballet shoes.

2. I never said we would bake a cake for the party.

3. Together, they ate pancakes for dinner.

4. You can join us on the dance floor!

5. I didn't see him digging up the rosebush!

6. Is it possible to take the test again?

7. She said the spending limit is twenty bucks.

8. Do you know who sent the package?

EXERCISE 4

Use each pronoun in a sentence. Then circle if it is
SINGULAR or PLURAL.

1. Me   Singular   Plural

2. You   Singular   Plural

3. They   Singular   Plural

4. I   Singular   Plural

5. We   Singular   Plural

6. Theirs   Singular   Plural

7. Her   Singular   Plural

8. Us   Singular   Plural

EXERCISE 5

Use a pronoun from the word bank to complete each sentence. Use each pronoun only once.

> me   they   its   who   mine   nobody
> you   everyone   his   what

1. _____ was able to complete the marathon.

2. Are all these gifts for _____?

3. _____ could believe it was snowing in July.

4. _____ gave you that cool hat?

5. _____ happened to the rug?

6. Connor is eating his jelly beans now, but I'll eat _____ later.

7. The diamond lost _____ shine.

8. Don't tell _____ what to do!

9. _____ got caught in the rain on their run.

10. Everyone forgot it was _____ birthday.

EXERCISE 6

Use a reflexive pronoun from the word bank to complete each sentence. Use each pronoun only once.

myself   himself   herself   yourself   itself
themselves   ourselves   yourselves

1. I found _____ thinking about the past more than ever.

2. They found the buried treasure hidden on the island, all by _____.

3. You need to do the math homework _____.

4. The acrobat practiced the routine by _____ several times a week.

5. We baked the birthday cake _____.

6. The bathrooms are new, but the school _____ was built more than 100 years ago.

7. The chef created the extensive menu _____.

8. You got _____ into this mess, so you have to get _____ out!
   ↖ For this question, use the same pronoun two times!

33

EXERCISE 7

Some of these sentences have an inappropriate shift. Write the type of inappropriate shift a sentence has on the line. Then rewrite the sentence to fix it. If the sentence is correct, mark it with a C.

Psst!! There are two kinds of inappropriate shifts: WRONG CASE and WRONG NUMBER.

1. Them went to the grocery store.   _____

2. I'm going to bring she along for the ride.   _____

3. I want to ride the roller coaster alone.   _____

4. Every time I eat pizza, we get pepperoni on it.   _____

5. She can't wait to see them at the cookout.   _____

6. The customer didn't know what they wanted.   ---------------------------

7. Help I pack my suitcase, please.   ---------------------------

8. If you need an extra pillow, they should ask.   ---------------------------

9. When I go to the movies, I get popcorn
with extra butter.   ---------------------------

10. Me found a giant rubber duck in the bathtub.   ---------------------------

EXERCISE 8

Underline the **COMPOUND PRONOUN** in each sentence. State if it is **CORRECT** or **INCORRECT**. If it is incorrect, rewrite the sentence correctly.

Psst! It's not always grammatically correct to use "I" instead of "me"!

1. Me and Jooahn are taking the bus.

2. The librarian and I recommend the book *Camp Quiltbag* by Nicole Melleby and A. J. Sass.

3. The haunted house scared Shaquana and I so badly, we screamed at the top of our lungs!

4. It's time for me and him to hit the hay.

5. Even though we are teenagers, me and Lisseth refuse to believe that Santa Claus isn't real.

BONUS QUESTION!
What kind of pronoun problems did you find in these sentences?

EXERCISE 9

Choose the correct pronoun for the compound pronoun in each sentence.

1. He / Him and Constance will present the award for best dressed.

2. My father and I / me sat front row at the World Series this year.

3. If they / them and Paula can solve the equation, our team will win the tournament.

4. Give the magazines to we / us and Fanny.

5. He / Him and Carlos got lost on the first day of school.

6. Kristos and me / I will catch the runaway chickens!

7. We / us and the campers can pitch the tents.

8. There were enough blankets for the family and me / I.

9. Abe and me / I will do all the laundry.

10. She / Her and her friends formed a mystery-solving club.

UNIT 1
Chapter 3: ACTIVE and PASSIVE VOICE

A **VERB** is a word used to describe an action.

When a verb is **ACTIVE**, the subject of the sentence is doing something.

Example:
    active verb
    Anita kicked the rusty can.

subject

Anita does something to the can.

When a verb is **PASSIVE**, something is done to the subject of the sentence.

Example:
    passive verb
    The rusty can was kicked by Anita.

subject

Something is done to the can.

If the verb is active, a sentence is in **ACTIVE VOICE**. Active voice is clear and direct.

Example:

Kamala listened to the podcast. ← ACTIVE VOICE

If the verb is passive, a sentence is in **PASSIVE VOICE**. Passive voice is often wordy and not as direct.

Example:

The podcast was listened to by Kamala ← PASSIVE VOICE

One verb can have different forms, called a **TENSE**. Verb tenses show when the action in a sentence takes place.

Verbs in **PAST TENSE** express an action that has already happened.

Example:

I helped my teacher take attendance this morning.

← past

Verbs in **PRESENT TENSE** express an action that is currently happening.

Example:

I help my teacher take attendance every day.

← present

Verbs in **FUTURE TENSE** express an action that has not happened yet.

Example:

I <u>will help</u> my teacher take attendance after the bell.

 future

Verbs can be passive or active in all tenses.

	ACTIVE	PASSIVE
PAST	Nirav closed the locker.	The locker was closed by Nirav.
PRESENT	Nirav closes the locker.	The locker is closed by Nirav.
FUTURE	Nirav will close the locker.	The locker will be closed by Nirav.

 PASSIVE VERBS

To make a verb passive, add a form of the verb "to be," such as **is**, **was**, or **will be**.

Tips for Using Active and Passive Voice

1. Using active voice is usually better than using passive voice. Active voice is clearer and more direct.

2. Don't shift from active to passive voice (or vice versa!) in the same sentence. Keep your verb voices consistent.

Examples:

✗ When Ollie <u>listened</u> to his walkie-talkie, strange voices <u>were heard</u>.

active voice

passive voice

Voices don't match!

✗ When the walkie-talkie <u>was listened</u> to, strange voices <u>were heard</u>.

passive voice

passive voice

Voices match! But passive voice makes the sentence awkward . . .

✓ When Ollie <u>listened</u> to his walkie-talkie, he <u>heard</u> strange voices.

active voice

active voice

Voices match and the sentence is strong!

EXERCISE 1

Underline the VERB in each sentence below. Then, decide if the sentence uses passive voice or active voice.

1. Serita uploaded the video to her Snapchat story. Passive Active

2. Piping-hot potato latkes were served by my mother. Passive Active

3. Diwali was celebrated by my family with fireworks, feasts, and fancy outfits! Passive Active

4. Colin tickled his little sister. Passive Active

5. The red envelopes were given to the children on Lunar New Year. Passive Active

6. Mrs. Phillips collected the algebra tests at exactly two o'clock. Passive Active

7. The pot of jjamppong was devoured by Mrs. Liu's guests. Passive Active

8. Jae read six volumes of their favorite manga series in one night! Passive Active

EXERCISE 2

Change each sentence from passive voice to active voice.

1. The crime scene was secured by the detective.

2. A snickerdoodle was eaten by the toddler.

3. Lex Luthor was captured by Superman.

4. A flower was tattooed on Jasmine's arm by the artist.

5. A selfie stick was used by Kennedy to take the picture.

6. The Notre-Dame cathedral was damaged by a fire.

7. Connie and Hunter were invited to the birthday party by James's dad.

8. The art museum was explored by Jonas for hours.

9. The team was led to victory by the quarterback.

10. The rowdy students were reprimanded by the principal.

Underline all the instances of PASSIVE VOICE in this passage. Then rewrite the passage in active voice.

The Hunger Games was written by Suzanne Collins. This dystopian book is enjoyed by young adults all around the world. In *The Hunger Games*, a nation of twelve districts, called Panem, is controlled by the Capitol. Each year, twenty-four district children are forced by the Capitol to compete in an event called the Hunger Games, where they fight to the death until only one is left standing. A lottery selects which kids will fight.

District 12 is lived in by the protagonist, Katniss Everdeen. When her younger sister, Prim, is selected by the lottery as tribute, Katniss volunteers to take her place. That year the baker's son Peeta is also chosen by the lottery. Katniss and Peeta are escorted to the Capitol by chaperones.

Before the Hunger Games begin, all the tributes train. As they train, the tributes are observed by game makers who want to assess their strengths and weaknesses. Tributes are also interviewed by Caesar Flickerman on national television. If a tribute's interview goes well, gifts from generous viewers might be sent to them to help them survive. When the games begin Katniss, Peeta, and the other tributes are tested by a series of life-threatening obstacles.

The light of day will only be seen by one winner.

EXERCISE 4

Fill in the missing sentence by changing the verb to the correct tense. Then state if the new verb is ACTIVE or PASSIVE.

1. Past tense: Drew hosted the baby shower.

   Present tense: Drew is hosting the baby shower.

   Future tense:

   Voice:

2. Past tense: The Oscar-winning film was produced by a brand-new studio.

   Present tense:

   Future tense: The Oscar-winning film will be produced by a brand-new studio.

   Voice:

3. Past tense:

   Present tense: Keyrin passes the naan around the table.

   Future tense: Keyrin will pass the naan around the table.

   Voice:

4. **Past tense:**

   Present tense: This pizzeria makes more than ten specialty pies.

   Future tense: This pizzeria will make more than ten specialty pies.

   Voice:

5. **Past tense:** The Saint Patrick's Day parade was so much fun.

   Present tense: The Saint Patrick's Day parade is so much fun.

   Future tense:

   Voice:

6. **Past tense:** Chicken empanadas were served by the food truck.

   Present tense:

   Future tense: Chicken empanadas will be served by the food truck.

   Voice:

EXERCISE 5

Change each sentence from active voice to passive voice.

1. The football team washed cars to raise money for new equipment.

2. Shelia wore her hoodie even though it was 90 degrees out.

3. Marius ordered five new science fiction books to read on vacation.

4. The five-year-old spilled paint on the brand-new living room rug.

5. The server delivered three burgers and three strawberry shakes to our table.

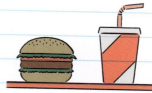

6. The student made a careless mistake on the exam.

7. Scientists have discovered three more melting glaciers in Antarctica.

8. After practice, the volleyball team devoured the tray of lasagna.

9. Beyoncé sang the national anthem at the Super Bowl.

10. The bakery donated four dozen apple pies to the camp.

BONUS QUESTION! What effect does passive voice have on the sentences? Are they stronger or weaker? Why, do you think?

EXERCISE 6

Decide whether each sentence is written in active voice or passive voice. Rewrite the sentences that use passive voice so they use active voice. If they need an active subject, add one.

1. Graffiti had been scrawled all over the building by the artist.　　Active　Passive

2. The class president has been elected.　　Active　Passive

3. After dinner, the dishes in the sink were washed and put away.

Active   Passive

4. Janet marathon-watched a full season of *Heartstopper* in one day.

Active   Passive

5. A rainbow bandana was worn by Monica.

Active   Passive

6. Mae added whipped cream and sprinkles to her banana split.

Active   Passive

7. Endangered species should always be protected.

Active   Passive

8. The quarterback sang a song in the locker-room shower.

Active   Passive

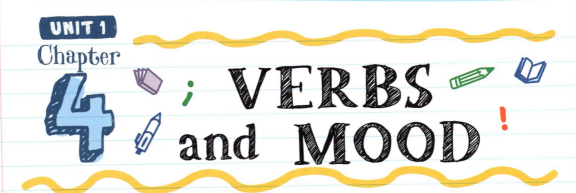

; VERBS and MOOD !

VERB MOODS tell us the attitude of the speaker.

There are five verb moods to know: indicative, imperative, interrogative, conditional, and subjunctive.

I. INDICATIVE verbs communicate facts, opinions, and statements. It is the verb mood we use most often.

Examples:

Hummingbirds are the only birds ← fact
that can fly backward.

I don't like that shade of blue. ← opinion

Eileen appreciated the get-well card. ← statement

2. IMPERATIVE verbs give commands or make requests.

Examples:

Please give me some space. ← request

Don't eat those rotten eggs! ← command

3. INTERROGATIVE verbs ask questions.

Examples:

How long will it take to drive to Alaska?

Did you pack an extra sandwich?

4. CONDITIONAL verbs describe what would happen if something else happens. Look for the words "if," "may," "should," and "could."

Examples:

If you leave the door open, the cat may sneak out.

She should feel better with a full eight hours of sleep.

5. SUBJUNCTIVE MOOD is used to express a hypothetical situation, wish, dream, hope, or desire, especially if the situation is unlikely or impossible. Look for suggestions, considerations, and the words "were" and "if."

Examples:

If I were a billionaire, I would end world hunger.

I wish it were the weekend already.

AVOID MOOD SHIFTS

Sentences that use one verb mood are stronger than sentences with verb mood shifts, so be consistent. If your sentence starts in one mood, it should stay in that mood.

             imperative   *indicative*

✗ Don't forget to feed the dogs, and you should take them for a walk.

✓ Don't forget to feed the dogs and take them for a walk.

                       imperative   *imperative*

             subjunctive   *indicative*

✗ If I were a mermaid, I will braid shells and seaweed into my hair.

✓ If I were a mermaid, I would braid shells and seaweed into my hair.

           subjunctive   *subjunctive*

Match each term to the correct definition.

1. Verb mood _____

2. Indicative mood _____

3. Imperative mood _____

4. Interrogative mood _____

5. Conditional mood _____

6. Subjunctive mood _____

7. Mood shift _____

A. Used to state a fact

B. Used to describe what could happen if something else happens

C. Use of two different moods in the same sentence

D. The manner or attitude in which the action in a sentence is expressed

E. Used to tell someone what to do

F. Used to describe wishes, dreams, or desires, whether possible or not

G. Used to ask a question

Change each present tense indicative verb phrase to the past and future tense.

PRESENT	PAST	FUTURE
1. I fly	-------------------	------------------
2. You gloat	-------------------	------------------
3. They clip	-------------------	------------------
4. He skips	-------------------	------------------
5. I stop	-------------------	------------------
6. You climb	-------------------	------------------
7. She teases	-------------------	------------------
8. I observe	-------------------	------------------
9. We shovel	-------------------	------------------
10. I rock	-------------------	------------------

EXERCISE 3

Write the mood of each verb on the line: indicative, imperative, interrogative, conditional, or subjunctive.

1. Will summer camp have color wars this year? _____

2. Help, I'm being chased by a chicken! _____

3. It is my fourteenth birthday today. _____

4. Did you buy the concert tickets in advance? _____

5. If my dog could talk, we would have great conversations. _____

6. If you save your money, you could buy a car one day. _____

7. I would like him more if he were nicer. _____

8. Get out of my way! _____

9. I wish I would never get older. _____

10. I live in a purple house with yellow polka dots. _____

EXERCISE 4

Fill in the two missing sentences using the correct verb mood. The first one is done for you.

1. Indicative: I like to go ice skating.

   Imperative: *Go ice skating with me!*

   Interrogative: *Do you like to go ice skating?*

2. Indicative:

   Imperative: Get out of the way!

   Interrogative:

3. Indicative:

   Imperative:

   Interrogative: Is this Lauren's bed?

4. Indicative:

   Imperative: Shut the television off!

   Interrogative:

5. Indicative: I went shopping.

   Imperative:

   Interrogative:

6. Indicative:

   Imperative:

   Interrogative: Did you eat your dinner?

7. Indicative:

   Imperative: Slow down, Susan!

   Interrogative:

8. Indicative:

   Imperative:

   Interrogative: Did Miriam tie her shoes?

9. Indicative:

   Imperative: Violet, use your calculator for math homework.

   Interrogative:

10. Indicative: You rested after the trip.

    Imperative:

    Interrogative:

EXERCISE 5

Identify the verb mood used in each sentence. Write C for conditional or S for subjunctive. Underline the words in each sentence that help you decide.

1. If I jump, that shark will bite me! _____

2. They would be a great babysitter if they liked kids. _____

3. If you get home past midnight, you will turn into a pumpkin! _____

4. I would speak Italian better if I practiced regularly. _____

5. If you leave me alone with this chocolate cake, there won't be any left when you get back! _____

6. I wish I could snap my fingers and shape-shift into a bird. _____

7. If I had every Pokémon card in print, my collection would be valuable. _____

8. If I had a time machine, I would visit the Jurassic Period and ride a stegosaurus! _____

EXERCISE 6

Write five sentences about a role model you admire using a different verb mood in each sentence.

MY ROLE MODEL IS:

Verb Mood	Sentence
Indicative	
Imperative	
Interrogative	
Conditional	
Subjunctive	

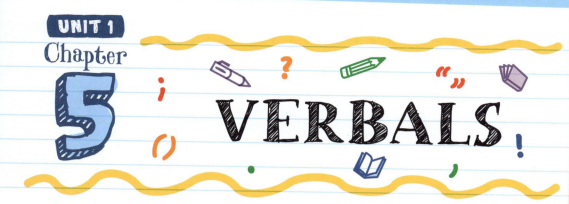

A **VERBAL** is a verb that acts as a different part of speech, like a noun or an adjective.

A **VERBAL PHRASE** is a phrase that begins with a verb or a verbal.

There are three kinds of verbals:

But not all words that end in -ing are gerunds!

1. A **GERUND** is a verb that acts as a noun. They can be used any way a noun can be used, including as the subject or the object of a sentence. All gerunds end in -ing.

Examples: The verbal is the subject.

Volunteering makes Julio feel happy.

The verbal is the object.

Julio loves volunteering.

A **GERUND PHRASE** is a phrase that begins with a gerund. (It still acts like a noun.)

Example:

Climbing over the fence is not as easy as it looks!

Cutting in line is usually rude.

a word that describes a noun

2. A **PARTICIPLE** is a verb that acts as an adjective.

A **PAST PARTICIPLE** modifies or describes a noun in the past tense. They usually end in -n, -en, -t, -ed, or -d.

Examples:

participle
▶ swollen eyes

participle
▶ broken noodles

A **PRESENT PARTICIPLE** describes a noun in the present tense. They always end in -ing.

Just add "-ing" to a verb!

Examples:

Sammi's eyes are swelling.
participle

Riley is breaking the noodles.
participle

A **PARTICIPLE PHRASE** is a phrase that begins with a participle. (It still acts like an adjective.)

Examples:

present participle phrase

Resting in the shade, Nonna didn't notice us.

past participle phrase

Locked in the tower, Rapunzel was bored.

3. An **INFINITIVE** is a verb form that always begins with "to." They can be used as nouns, adjectives, or adverbs.

Examples:

Jamal needs <u>to sit</u>. ← acts like a noun

Priya went to the library <u>to study</u>. ← acts like an adverb

Rocky road is the best flavor <u>to pick</u>. ← acts like an adjective

An **INFINITIVE PHRASE** is a phrase that begins with an infinitive. (It still acts like a noun, adjective, or adverb.)

Examples:
acts like a noun

<u>To act on Broadway</u> was Zulia's childhood dream.

acts like an adverb

The paramedics arrived <u>to help the child</u>.

Abuela showed me the best way <u>to make empanadas</u>.

acts like an adjective

EXERCISE 1

Match each term to the correct definition.

1. A verb that acts like an adjective. _____

2. A verb that acts like a noun. _____

3. A verbal that describes a noun in the present tense. _____

4. A verb that begins with "to." _____

5. A verb that acts as a different part of speech, like a noun or an adjective. _____

6. A verbal that describes a noun in the past tense. _____

7. A phrase that begins with a verb acting as a different part of speech. _____

8. A phrase that begins with a verb acting like a noun. _____

9. A phrase that begins with an infinitive. _____

10. A phrase beginning with a verb that acts like an adjective. _____

A. Infinitive

B. Participle

C. Verbal

D. Present participle

E. Verbal phrase

F. Gerund phrase

G. Past participle

H. Infinitive phrase

I. Gerund

J. Participle phrase

EXERCISE 2

Underline the **GERUND** in each sentence. If the sentence has a **GERUND PHRASE**, circle it.

1. Exercising is good for your body and your mind.

2. I love baking pecan pies on Thanksgiving!

3. You might be sorry, but apologizing is not enough this time.

4. At the assembly, the students learned that vaping is dangerous.

5. When she got caught, Laurie realized that cheating is not the answer.

6. Now that she is in high school, Chloe is trying to improve her grades.

7. Would you mind training my dog to do tricks?

8. While abroad, we noticed that speaking multiple languages is helpful.

9. Keke knew that memorizing her lines would be difficult.

10. Practicing your card tricks makes you a better magician.

EXERCISE 3

Complete each sentence by adding a gerund or a gerund phrase.

REMEMBER: Gerunds end in –ing!

1. My favorite winter activity is _____.

2. _____ too many gummy bears in one sitting can give you a stomachache.

3. _____ fireworks on the Fourth of July is exciting!

4. When you pay attention in class, _____ good grades is not as hard as you think.

5. _____ a little each day helped the students ace their tests.

6. _____ in front of a crowd can be terrifying!

7. This summer vacation, _____ to juggle five balls at once is Shanae's goal.

8. _____ before you cross the street can keep you safe.

9. If you have a problem, _____ with your friends can help.

10. _____ at the amusement park is boring!

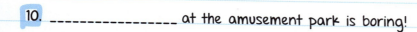

EXERCISE 4

In the sentences below, underline the GERUNDS or GERUND PHRASES being used as a subject.

Psst! Not all gerunds and gerund phrases will be underlined!

1. Singing in the shower is a great way to start the morning.

2. Luca hates mowing the lawn.

3. Playing Candy Crush can be addictive.

4. Reading is my favorite rainy-day activity.

5. Why don't you like fishing?

6. Finding a lost hamster in your house can be tricky!

7. They like listening to K-pop when they clean their room.

8. Painting is harder than it looks!

9. I'm too tired to go hiking today.

10. Making friends in a new school takes time.

EXERCISE 5

Underline the **PARTICIPLE** in each sentence. Circle **PAST** if it is a past participle or **PRESENT** if it is a present participle.

1. Aaliyah's tattered scarf is falling apart.   Past   Present

2. Jada kept the crew waiting.   Past   Present

3. Terrence looked worried when he started the pop quiz.   Past   Present

4. When the car hit the curb, the front tire was damaged.   Past   Present

5. We felt exhausted after the long plane ride.   Past   Present

6. Tony's plan seems confusing.   Past   Present

7. Nova was invited to the party, but she didn't want to go.

Past   Present

8. The frozen pond was perfect for playing hockey.

Past   Present

9. The burnt toast was inedible.

Past   Present

10. The substitute was fired because he fell asleep on the job!

Past   Present

16 × 24   23 × 12
12 × 15   7 × 23
26 × 22   21 × 18
17 × 28   11 × 29

Write a sentence using each verb as a past participle.

1. Bake

2. Ruin

3. Find

4. Haunt

5. Sauté

6. Break

7. Write

8. Take

EXERCISE 7

For each sentence below, underline the **PARTICIPLE PHRASE** and draw an arrow to the noun it modifies.

1. Listening to the radio, Uncle Al fell asleep.

2. The chicken roasting in the oven smelled delicious.

3. The man searching the mansion can't find his diamond earring.

4. The girl wearing purple Crocs is my cousin.

5. The couple walking along the beach held hands.

6. Ripped at the knee, the jeans were old.

7. Glazed with icing, the cinnamon buns cooled.

8. Shouting with happiness, the children opened their gifts.

EXERCISE 8

In each sentence below, determine if the teal words form a **GERUND** phrase or a **PRESENT PARTICIPLE** phrase. Write the answer on the line.

1. Learning a foreign language takes time. _____

2. The presenter was speaking from the heart. _____

3. Packing for a trip can be an overwhelming task. _____

4. Complaining of headache, Timo goes to bed. _____

5. Exiting the pool, Frank slips on the wet floor. _____

6. Making the honor roll is something to be proud of. _____

7. Tonya's voice was dazzling the audience. _____

8. Looking through a microscope can be surprising. _____

9. Radhika was painting her toenails when she spilled the nail polish. _____

10. Traveling abroad is always an adventure! _____

EXERCISE 9

Add an infinitive or infinitive phrase to complete each sentence.

1. Saul was eager _____ surfing.

2. I am learning _____ macaroons.

3. Alicia was ready _____ to the city.

4. Diego offered _____ the dessert.

5. Jules likes _____ by herself.

6. The students were amazed _____ a pupa in the praying mantis's tank.

7. The acrobats were trying _____ a new routine.

8. My auntie taught me how _____ a bike.

9. Crystal put on her coat _____ a walk.

10. Abuela hopes _____ us over the summer.

REMEMBER:
An infinitive is a verb that starts with "to," like "to be."

EXERCISE 10

Underline the **INFINITIVE PHRASE** in each sentence. Write the part of speech it acts as on the line.

Psst! An infinitive phrase never acts like a verb!

1. Would you like to work together? _____

2. The actors were ready to rehearse the death scene. _____

3. To become a member of the National Honor Society, you must get good grades. _____

4. In my family it is tradition to make ravioli on Christmas. _____

5. Do you have the motivation to train for a marathon? _____

6. Madison wants to build the set for the play. _____

7. The athletes were thrilled to make the playoffs. ---------------------------

8. Ramneet's chore is to take out the trash. ---------------------------

9. The group got tickets to see the circus. ---------------------------

10. Tricia needed someone to feed her fish when ---------------------------
    she was at camp.

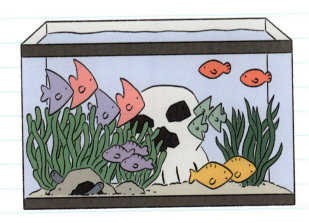

DEFINING FROM CONTEXT

CONTEXT is the circumstances around a situation or event that can shed light on its meaning. You can use context to figure out the meaning of an unfamiliar word or phrase.

Also called context clues!

Example:

context →

To get to Piccadilly Circus, walk to the station on the corner and take the Tube three stops.

HUH?? →

← context

THINK:

If you don't know what "the Tube" is, you can use context clues from the sentence to figure it out. The words "station" and "stops" help you realize it's a train, like the subway in New York City or the Metro in Paris!

UNDERGROUND

You can use context to figure out the meaning of an unfamiliar word or phrase in a **fiction text**. The information surrounding it, and the words you *do* know, are clues to its meaning.

Example:

We lived on Waverly Place, in a warm, clean, two-bedroom flat that sat *context* above a small Chinese bakery specializing in steamed pastries and dim sum. In the early morning, when the alley was still quiet, I could smell *context* *fragrant* *HUH??* red beans as they were cooked down to a pasty *context* sweetness.

—Amy Tan, *The Joy Luck Club*

What does the word **fragrant** mean? If you're not sure, look for context clues in the passage:

▶ Fragrant is used to describe the scent of red beans.

▶ The narrator describes the red bean smell as sweet.

▶ The narrator smells the red beans from her apartment, above the bakery.

So, **fragrant** likely means a strong, pleasant smell.

Context clues can also help you understand **nonfiction texts**.

Example:

> In the afternoon of that day, we reached Annapolis, the capital of the State.
> *context* → It was the first large town that I had ever seen. I thought it a wonderful place ← *context*
>
> for its size—more ***imposing*** even than the Great House Farm! ← *context*
> ← HUH??
>
> —Frederick Douglass,
> *Narrative of the Life of Frederick Douglass*

To figure out what the word **imposing** means, look at the context clues around it:

▶ Douglass describes Annapolis as a "large" town and "wonderful" place.

← here "great" means "big"

▶ He observes Annapolis is bigger than the Great House Farm, the plantation where he was once enslaved.

Imposing likely means big, impressive, and grand!

EXERCISE 1

Use context clues to choose the correct definition for each word in teal.

1. Charlie realized she forgot to do the reading ten minutes before the bell! She was grateful for the short story's brevity.

   A. Intensity
   B. Concise use of words
   C. Humor
   D. Beautiful language

2. After a long soccer practice, Simon got out of the shower feeling relaxed and revitalized.

   A. Exhausted
   B. Moody
   C. Strengthened
   D. Fortunate

3. Mason struggled to write his research paper because there was a dearth of reliable sources on gumball machines.

   A. Scarcity
   B. Wealth
   C. Abundance
   D. Rarity

Psst! Context clues can be synonyms, antonyms, or other details that help explain the word.

4. After how she mistreated you, don't delude yourself into thinking Marcy is a good friend.

   A. Trap
   B. Fool
   C. Correct
   D. Fix

5. Marisa looked put together, but it was just a facade, hiding her true pain.

   A. Hard process
   B. Easy solution
   C. False appearance
   D. Medical problem

6. The teacher admonished the students for snickering during Jordan's presentation.

   A. Praised
   B. Scolded
   C. Taunted
   D. Belittled

7. I could tell Stephanie was angry when she showed up to practice with a glower on her face.

   A. Smile
   B. Tattoo
   C. Bruise
   D. Scowl

8. My broken arm will be an impediment to making the lacrosse team this season.

    A. Obstacle

    B. Joke

    C. Opportunity

    D. Experience

9. Stacy's amiable nature meant she had no problem making friends.

    A. Sneaky

    B. Academic

    C. Immature

    D. Pleasant

10. When Elizabeth's father lost his job, her family was extra frugal with their money.

    A. Scared

    B. Careful

    C. Greedy

    D. Irresponsible

EXERCISE 2

Use context to define the teal word in each sentence.
Underline the context you used to determine its meaning.

1. If parents gave their children an allowance at the end of the week,
   children would have an incentive to help around the house.

2. Jenna approached the roller coaster with trepidation after hearing
   screams of terror from other riders.

3. Pauline met her parents' lofty expectations by excelling in all her classes,
   mastering trombone and piano, starring in the winter musical, and running
   for class president.

4. After Suzanne mediated a fight between her two best friends, everyone
   enjoyed going out for ice cream together.

5. The tennis team's lucrative after-school bake sale raised enough money to replace thirty rackets for the upcoming season.

6. Theresa loathes cheese because it smells stinky and gives her a terrible stomachache.

7. Ling, an adept mah-jongg player, has learned many helpful strategies from her grandmother.

8. When Mrs. Breen questioned Phil about his tardiness, he quickly fabricated an elaborate excuse.

9. The boisterous crowd stomped their feet and chanted Serena Williams's name as she emerged on the court.

10. As Molly flaunted her new Gucci bag, her friends and frenemies stared enviously.

EXERCISE 3

Use each vocabulary word in a sentence, and include at least one context clue that could help a reader figure out the word's definition.

vocab word · part of speech · definition

1. Erratic (adj) Inconsistent

2. Flourish (v) To grow or develop in a healthy way

3. Abate (v) To lessen, reduce, become smaller

4. Longevity (n) Long life or existence

5. **Benign** *(adj)* Gentle, kind, not harmful

6. **Usurp** *(v)* To take a position by force or illegally

7. **Haughty** *(adj)* Arrogant or disdainful

8. **Affluent** *(adj)* Wealthy

9. **Obstruct** *(v)* To block, prevent, hinder

10. **Terse** *(adj)* Curt, brief in words

Use context clues to define the underlined words in this passage. Then pick a synonym you could use to replace them.

More than ever, teenagers around the world, like the renowned activist Greta Thunberg, are speaking out about important issues.

In Canada, Autumn Peltier is known as the "water warrior." She is an Indigenous rights advocate from the Wikwemikong First Nation who has gained worldwide recognition for her work as a conservationist. From an early age, she was cognizant of the dangers of water pollution. During a water ceremony on a First Nation reserve, Peltier saw an advisory warning that the water was toxic. This motivated her to become a water rights activist, and she is adamant that all people should have access to clean drinking water. She was a keynote speaker at the 2018 United Nations World Water Day, has been named a water protector by the Assembly of First Nations, and has been nominated for the International Children's Peace Prize three times.

In Curitiba, Brazil, teenage environmental activist Kauá Rodolfo is leading a tree-planting initiative with Plant-for-the-Planet. Its motto, "Stop Talking, Start Planting," hopes to inspire people to save the environment by planting trees. Plant-for-the-Planet campaigns have planted more than one million trees worldwide.

And in Mali, Maimouna N'diaye encourages other young women to learn about science. As the youngest member of the award-winning national robotics team, N'diaye is a skilled coder and fervent promoter of STEM education. Her goals include starting her own programming company and using artificial intelligence to create an android capable of doing chores.

These remarkable teen advocates prove that with motivation and a mission, you can make change in the world at any age!

1. Renowned

synonym: _____

2. Advocate

synonym: _____

3. Cognizant

synonym: _____

4. Adamant

synonym: _____

5. **Initiative**

synonym: _____

6. **Fervent**

synonym: _____

EXERCISE 5

Grab the book that is closest to you (or any book you like). Read a page and pick out four words you don't know. Use context clues to guess their meaning. Then check your answers by looking the words up in a dictionary.

1. word:
   definition:

2. word:
   definition:

3. word:
   definition:

4. word:
   definition:

UNIT 1
Chapter 7
AFFIXES and ROOTS

A **ROOT** is a word or portion of a word from which other words can grow. It reflects the word's core meaning.

AFFIXES are attached to the beginning or end of a root to modify its meaning.

A **PREFIX** is an affix that is attached to the beginning of a word. A **SUFFIX** is an affix that is attached to the end of a word.

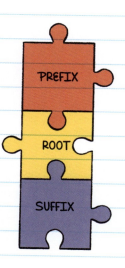

Example:
- Kind: having a friendly or considerate nature
  — root
- Unkind: not having a friendly or considerate nature
  — a prefix meaning "not"
- Kindness: the quality of being kind or considerate
  — a suffix meaning "state or quality"

The words "unkind" and "kindness" have the same root: "kind."

ROOTS AND AFFIXES

Even the words affix, prefix, and suffix have roots and affixes. Fix is the root word. It means "to be attached to something else."

in addition to
AFFIX

before
PREFIX

below
SUFFIX

Many English roots and affixes come from Latin and Greek.

Example:

Bi is a Latin root that means twice or doubly.

▶ Bicentennial: the two-hundredth anniversary of an event

▶ Bicep: a two-headed muscle in the arm

▶ Bicycle: a vehicle composed of two wheels

If you learn the most common roots and affixes, you can make educated guesses regarding the meaning of thousands of unfamiliar words!

Here are some common roots and affixes to know:

ROOT/ AFFIX	TRANSLATION	EXAMPLE	LANGUAGE
Astro	Star	**Astronomy:** the study of everything in the universe beyond Earth's atmosphere	Greek
Chron	Time	**Chronological:** a record of events starting with the earliest and following the order in which they occurred	Greek
Cycl	Circle or wheel	**Bicycle:** a vehicle with two wheels	Greek
Dem	People	**Democracy:** a system of government where people elect representatives	Greek
Gen	Birth, or race	**Generation:** the creation or production of something	Latin
Geo	Earth	**Geography:** the study of the Earth's physical features	Greek

ROOT/ AFFIX	TRANSLATION	EXAMPLE	LANGUAGE
Hydro	Water	Hydroplane: a light, fast motorboat designed to skim over the surface of water	Greek
Hypno	Sleep	Hypnotize: to induce a calm, focused state in oneself or another person	Greek
Ject	Throw	Eject: to force or throw something out in a violent way	Latin
Magni	Big	Magnify: to make something look larger than it is	Greek
Mech	Machine	Mechanical: working or produced by machines or machinery	Greek
Mis	Send	Missile: an object that is forcibly propelled at a target	Latin

ROOT/ AFFIX	TRANSLATION	EXAMPLE	LANGUAGE
Ology	Study	Zoology: the scientific study of animals	Greek
Phobos	Fear or horror	Phobia: An excessive fear of something or aversion to something	Greek
Phon	Sound	Telephone: a system for transmitting voices over a distance using wire or radio	Greek
Port	Carry	Import: to bring goods or services into a country from abroad for sale	Latin
Scope	See	Telescope: an instrument that allows people to see distant objects	Greek
Terr	Earth	Terrestrial: things related to the planet Earth	Latin

EXERCISE 1

Draw a line connecting each root to its definition.

terr	star
mis	study
hypno	against
anti	Earth
ology	birth
gen	throw
port	sleep
astro	people
ject	send
dem	carry

EXERCISE 2

What English words contain the roots listed below? Name at least three words for each root.

Psst! Use the root definitions from the chart on pages 98–100 to get started.

1. Astro

2. Ject

3. Ology

4. Port

5. Mis

6. Magni

7. Scope

8. Dem

9. Phobos

10. Chron

11. Cycl

12. Geo

13. Hydro

14. Mech

15. Phon

EXERCISE 3

Practice using affixes and roots to figure out meaning.

1. List five words that use the suffix –ful.

    How are the definitions of these five words similar?

    What do you think the suffix –ful means?

2. List five words that use the prefix re-.

    How are the definitions of these five words similar?

What do you think the prefix re- means?

means the "study of" or "account of"

3. Below are four words that contain the root "ology." Underline the other ROOT or AFFIX in each word. Using your prior knowledge of these words, what do you think each root or affix means?

Psst! If you're stuck, use a dictionary!

Biology

Geology

Dermatology

Psychology

EXERCISE 4

Underline the **ROOT** in each word listed below. Use your knowledge of the root's meaning and the affix to write a definition for the word. The first one is done for you.

1. Triangle   *A shape with three angles*

2. Unwind

3. Abandonment

4. Portable

5. Preview

6. Encouragement

7. Colorful

8. Cheerless

9. Reliable

10. Unhappy

EXERCISE 5

Underline the AFFIX in each word listed below. Then state if it is a PREFIX or a SUFFIX.

1. Disadvantage _____

2. Companion _____

3. Preventable _____

4. Improper _____

5. Rewrite _____

6. Nonsense _____

7. Cardiac _____

8. Premade _____

9. Unkind _____

10. Helpless _____

EXERCISE 6

The paragraph below contains many words with the same prefix. This prefix means "forward" or "for." CIRCLE all the words that share this prefix, then answer the questions below.

Do you ever procrastinate before starting a task? Many people struggle with deadlines, so chances are you probably have. Perhaps you've waited until the night before a project was due to start working on it. Delaying progress on an unenjoyable task is a common problem for teenagers and adults alike. Studies have proven that procrastination can produce a great deal of anxiety and stress. Research also shows that procrastination can be "particularly pronounced in students" (Cherry 2022). *Psychological Bulletin* found that a whopping 80% to 95% of college students procrastinate on a regular basis (Steel 2007), particularly when it comes to completing assignments and coursework. Experts offer promising advice: To promote productivity and avoid getting off task, it helps to be proactive. Before you proceed, eliminate distractions and set goals. This process may prove to help you keep your promises!

1. What is the prefix?

2. Use your knowledge of roots and affixes to define one of the words you circled.

3. How does its definition relate to the meaning of the prefix?

EXERCISE 7

Underline the **ROOT** of each word in teal. Use context clues to write a definition of each root.

1. An aquarium is a tank where underwater plants and animals are kept.

2. Circumference is the distance around something.

3. Malignant means hostile, cruel, or harmful.

4. Aquaphobia is the fear of water.

5. A dictionary is a resource that lists and provides meanings of words.

6. A factory is a place where goods are manufactured.

7. A pesticide is a chemical or substance to kill pests.

8. A thermometer is a tool for measuring a temperature.

9. A monologue is a long speech by one person.

10. An autobiography is an account of someone's life written by that person.

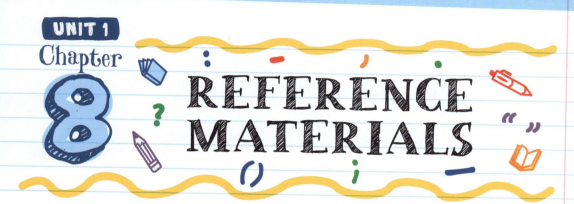

REFERENCE MATERIALS

REFERENCE MATERIALS are sources you can use to find answers to your questions.

A **DICTIONARY** is a reference book or an online resource that lists words and their **DEFINITIONS**.

> **DEFINITION**
> the meaning of a word, symbol, or sign

A physical dictionary lists words in **ALPHABETICAL ORDER**.

? ALPHABETICAL ORDER

Alphabetical order means arranging words in the order of the alphabet: A words first, B words second, and so on:

<u>A</u>djective, <u>N</u>oun, <u>P</u>ronoun, <u>V</u>erb

If two words start with the same letter, look at the second letter. If the second letter is the same, look at the third letter, and so on.:

<u>Al</u>batross, <u>Al</u>ligator, <u>An</u>t, <u>An</u>teater, <u>An</u>telope

Most dictionaries provide **seven** key pieces of information:

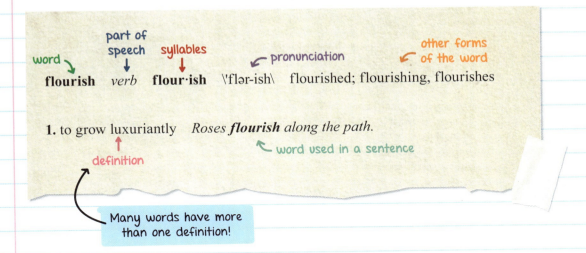

word →
flourish

part of
speech
↓
verb

syllables
↓
flour·ish

← pronunciation
\'flər-ish\

other forms
of the word ↰
flourished; flourishing, flourishes

1. to grow luxuriantly   *Roses **flourish** along the path.*
↑
definition

↳ word used in a sentence

Many words have more
than one definition!

PRONUNCIATION is the way a word
is said aloud.

A **PRONUNCIATION GUIDE** provides
the phonetic spelling of a word using a
combination of symbols and characters to
show how it can be sounded out.

Most online dictionaries
have a "read aloud"
function that plays the
pronunciation out loud!

▶ Anemone \ə-'ne-mə-nē\

▶ Quinoa \'kēn-'wä\

A **SYLLABLE** is a single, unbroken sound within a word.
Understanding syllables helps you pronounce words.

A **GLOSSARY** is an alphabetical list of definitions in the back of a book or textbook. Glossaries list words used in the book that are specific to the topic.

Example:

In an astronomy textbook, the glossary might include the words **equinox**, **galaxy**, and **meteor**.

A **THESAURUS** is a reference book or online resource that provides a list of **SYNONYMS** for words. Thesaurus entries can be really long, and the synonyms aren't listed in alphabetical order.

SYNONYM
a word or phrase that has the same or similar meaning as another word or phrase

Example:

reference word
part of speech
synonyms

good *(adjective)* fine, excellent, superb, magnificent, terrific, outstanding, great, marvelous, superior, acceptable, exceptional, splendid, awesome, fantastic, tremendous, wonderful, first-rate, brilliant

The movie was good.
. . . excellent!
. . . outstanding!
. . . marvelous!

You can use a thesaurus to:

▶ Expand your vocabulary

▶ Avoid repeating the same word in a sentence or paragraph

▶ Help you remember the word that's on the tip of your tongue

▶ Find the exact word for what you mean

THINK:

Not all synonyms have the exact same definition. The words "smart" and "brilliant" and "precocious" are synonyms, but they mean slightly different things.

smart = having intelligence

brilliant = having a LOT of intelligence

precocious = having intelligence at a young age

EXERCISE 1

Use a thesaurus to find three synonyms for each word below.

1. Evil _____ _____ _____

2. Skill _____ _____ _____

3. Powerful _____ _____ _____

4. Thoughtful _____ _____ _____

5. Rude _____ _____ _____

6. Sneaky _____ _____ _____

7. Enthusiastic _____ _____ _____

8. Lonely _____ _____ _____

9. Stinky _____ _____ _____

10. Hard _____ _____ _____

EXERCISE 2

Circle whether each statement about reference materials is TRUE or FALSE. If a statement is false, rewrite it to make it true.

1. You can find a word's part of speech in a dictionary.

   True   False

2. If you want to find the definition of a biology term in your biology textbook, you should use a thesaurus.

   True   False

3. Multiple definitions of a word can be found in a dictionary.

   True   False

4. You want to find a word to replace "special."
   You should use a thesaurus.   True   False

5. All words have one syllable.   True   False

6. A pronunciation guide can help you sound out   True   False
   "onomatopoeia."

7. You see \'kər-nəl\ next to the word "colonel."   True   False
   This tells you the word's part of speech.

8. A glossary usually appears at the beginning of a text.   True   False

9. A pronunciation guide tells you a word's origin.   True   False

10. This entry would be found in a thesaurus: True   False
    pretty (adj) beautiful, gorgeous, lovely.

EXERCISE 3

For each situation below, decide which reference material to use: thesaurus, dictionary, or glossary.

1. Your English teacher asks you to define all the words you don't know in an article your class is reading.

2. In your foreign language class, you are giving a presentation about foods from around the world, but you aren't sure how to pronounce some of the words.

3. You are doing research on DNA. You don't know some of the terms used in the textbook you are reading. Where would you find their meanings?

4. You are surprised to learn that the word "novel" has multiple meanings. Where do you find out more?

5. You are writing a personal essay about your summer vacation. You don't want to use the word "trip" again.

6. You don't know what the word "onerous" means.

7. You want to find synonyms for the word "challenging."

8. You would like to know how to say "camaraderie."

9. You are reading a book on fishing. You already know what bait, rods, and sinkers are. However, you come across a word you don't know—"chumming." Where could you find out more about this term?

10. You're writing a thank-you letter to your teacher. You've already used the word "thanks." You need another word to replace it.

EXERCISE 4

Use words in the word bank to label the parts of each dictionary entry. Each word will be used at least once per entry. Some words will be used more than once.

> entry word   part of speech   syllables   pronunciation
> guide   definition   example sentence

Entry Word

Syllables

Part of Speech

Pronunciation

Definition

Example sentence

Part of Speech

Definition

mutiny *(noun)* mu·ti·ny | \'myü-tə-nē\ : forcible or passive resistance to lawful authority *especially*: concerted revolt (as of a naval crew) against discipline or a superior officer *The sailors staged a **mutiny** and took control of the ship.*

(verb) : to rise against or refuse to obey or observe authority

conscientious *(adjective)* con·sci·en·tious | \ˌkän(t)-shē-'en(t)-shəs\ **1**: meticulous, careful **2**: governed by or conforming to the dictates of conscience: scrupulous *He was a **conscientious** public servant.*

despondent *(adjective)* de·spon·dent | \di-'spän-dənt\ : feeling or showing extreme discouragement, dejection, or depression   *He was **despondent** about his health.*

pernicious *(adjective)* per·ni·cious | \pər-'ni-shəs\ **1:** highly injurious or destructive **2:** deadly   *She thinks television has a **pernicious** influence on our children.*

zephyr *(noun)* zeph·yr | \'ze-fər\ **1a:** a breeze from the west **b:** a gentle breeze   *Windsurfers lean into the prevailing southwestern **zephyr** at incredible speeds.*   **2:** any of various lightweight fabrics and articles of clothing

EXERCISE 5

Use a dictionary to complete the exercise below.

1. According to the dictionary, what is the meaning of **apex**?

2. How many definitions does the dictionary provide for the word **erratic**?

3. What part of speech is the word **exacerbate**?

4. What is the noun form of the word **exacerbate**?

5. Copy down the pronunciation key for the word **ignominious**.

6. According to the dictionary, how many syllables make up the word **ignominious**?

7. How many definitions are there for the word **petulant**?

8. Copy the dictionary's example sentence for the word **petulant**.

9. Inspired by the dictionary sentence, create your own sentence using **petulant**.

10. According to the dictionary, what is the plural form of **curriculum**?

EXERCISE 6

Some words have more than one definition. Choose the best definition for the word in teal.

1. Sonia came up with a novel idea to save the bookstore.

   A. a narrative prose dealing with the human experience
   B. new or unusual in an interesting way

2. Did Max harbor resentment after Sid forgot his birthday?

   A. to provide shelter
   B. to hold on to a thought or feeling

3. Ida B. Wells was a champion of women's rights.

   A. one that has defeated or surpassed all rivals in a competition
   B. a supporter or defender of a cause

4. As a teenager, you should be able to discriminate between right and wrong.

   A. to make a clear distinction
   B. to act based on prejudice

5. The pasta recipe called for brown butter and sage.

   A. a cooking herb
   B. a person well known for their wisdom

6. The refugees from Ukraine were seeking asylum in the United States.

   A. an institution for people with mental health conditions
   B. protection or immunity

7. Cathy approached the stray dog in a gentle and deliberate manner.

   A. leisurely or slow
   B. done or said on purpose

8. The eighth-graders were in buoyant spirits as they signed one another's yearbooks.

   A. able to float
   B. animated or excited

9. There was so much static in the background that Jenna had a hard time hearing her dad on the phone.

   A. noise in a receiver caused by electrical disturbance
   B. showing little change

10. Chess is a game that requires a great deal of concentration.

    A. the act or power of focusing
    B. a close gathering of people or things

Use a dictionary to define the bold words in this passage from Edgar Allan Poe's short story "The Black Cat."

For the most wild, yet most **homely** narrative which I am about to pen, I neither expect nor **solicit** belief. Mad indeed would I be to expect it, in a case where my very senses reject their own evidence. Yet, mad am I not—and very surely do I not dream. But to-morrow I die, and to-day I would unburden my soul. My immediate purpose is to place before the world, plainly, **succinctly**, and without comment, a series of mere household events. In their consequences, these events have terrified—have tortured—have destroyed me. Yet I will not attempt to **expound** them. To me, they have presented little but Horror—to many they will seem less terrible than baroques. Hereafter, perhaps, some intellect may be found which will reduce my **phantasm** to the common-place—some intellect more calm, more logical, and far less excitable than my own, which will perceive, in the circumstances I detail with awe, nothing more than an ordinary succession of very natural causes and effects.

From my infancy I was noted for the **docility** and humanity of my **disposition**. I was especially fond of animals, and was indulged by my parents with a great variety of pets. With these I spent most of my time, and never was so happy as when feeding and caressing them. This peculiarity of character grew with my growth, and in my manhood, I derived from it one of my principal sources of pleasure. To those who have cherished an affection for a faithful and **sagacious** dog, I need hardly be at the trouble of explaining the nature or the intensity of the gratification thus **derivable**. There is something in the unselfish and self-sacrificing love of a brute, which goes directly to the heart of him who has had frequent occasion to test the **paltry** friendship and gossamer fidelity of mere Man.

1. Homely

2. Solicit

3. Succinctly

4. Expound

5. Phantasm

6. Docility

7. Disposition

8. Sagacious

9. Derivable

10. Paltry

EXERCISE 8

Put all the B words below in alphabetical order.

bequeath   burgeon   boisterous   bygone   baffle
beckon   beguile   blaze   bravado   banter

Put all the O words in alphabetical order.

optimistic   originate   observant   occur   original
oodles   overflow   outfox   otherworldly   ornament

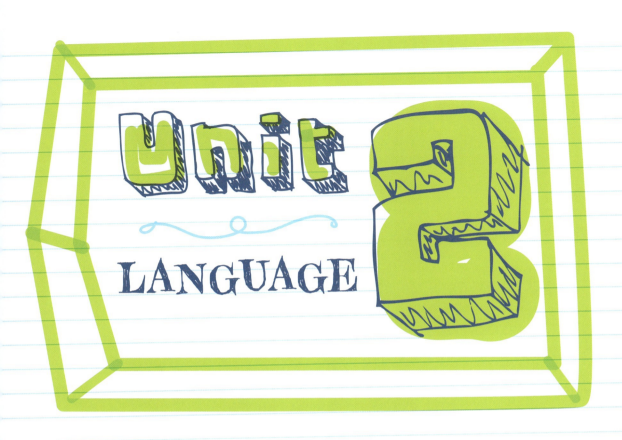

Unit 2

LANGUAGE

LANGUAGE is how we communicate. It's the way we use words and symbols to talk or write, and it's the way we play with meaning to be creative, persuasive, funny, or serious.

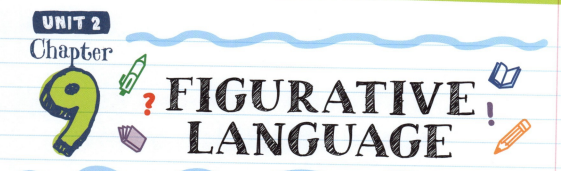

FIGURATIVE LANGUAGE

FIGURATIVE LANGUAGE is words or phrases that are used to convey a meaning that is different from their literal meaning. There are many kinds of figurative language.

An **IDIOM** is a commonly understood phrase that uses figurative language to say or describe something. Even though the words aren't literal, everyone still knows what you mean!

Examples:

It's raining cats and dogs! ← It's raining hard!

That was a piece of cake. ← Something was easy to do.

Hold your horses! ← Be patient!

I am under the weather. ← I am sick.

A **METAPHOR** directly compares two things by saying something is something else. Metaphors let writers add imagery and meaning to a sentence, with fewer words.

Example:

Life is a roller coaster.

A **SIMILE** indirectly compares two things using the word like or as.

Examples:

Life is like a roller coaster.

Your eyes are as blue as the ocean.

 **THINK:**

Is life LITERALLY a roller coaster? No! Is it literally LIKE a roller coaster? Also no! But comparing life to a roller coaster conveys the meaning that life is full of ups and downs and can feel both scary and exciting!

PERSONIFICATION is using human characteristics to describe nonhuman things.

Examples:

not a human!

The house groaned as we entered.

a human noise!

The alarm clock wailed.

As I ran through the field,
the grass tickled my feet.

An **ALLUSION** is a reference to a well-known story or event from history, literature, mythology, or religion.

Examples:

religious allusion to the biblical story of Adam and Eve

The answer key was like a serpent tempting Lisa to cheat on the test.

mythological allusion to the Roman god

The moment she saw Sara, Cupid's arrow pierced her heart.

To read or not to read, that is the question.

literary allusion to Shakespeare's Hamlet

How could you stab me in the back like that!?

historical allusion to Brutus's betrayal of Caesar

A **PUN** is a play on words that uses the various meanings of a word, or similar-sounding words, to create a funny effect.

Examples:

How do you scramble eggs? Beat them!

It's hard to <u>beat</u> scrambled eggs for breakfast!

When the ice cream parlor caught fire, the reporter got the <u>scoop</u>.

What's a serving of ice cream called? A scoop!

The astronauts had a <u>blast</u> on their trip to space.

What does a rocket do? Blast off!

HYPERBOLE is extreme or unrealistic exaggeration used for humor or emphasis.

Examples:

My shoes are killing me!

I'm so hungry I could eat a horse.

I've told you to clean your room a million times!

ONOMATOPOEIA is when a word sounds like the noise it refers to.

Examples:

▶ Buzz, moo, quack, honk, crackle, sizzle, swish, crash, bang, pow!

EXERCISE 1

Use figurative language to turn these boring, literal sentences into fun, descriptive ones! The first one is done for you.

1. Tina is mean.

   idiom

   Tina has a heart of stone.

2. Reading the textbook was boring.

3. When Julissa heard the bad news, she was overwhelmed.

4. I am very tired.

5. The raindrops hit the tin roof.

6. When we saw the painting, we all agreed: Todd is a great artist.

EXERCISE 2

Decide whether each sentence is a **SIMILE** or a **METAPHOR**. Write your answer on the line.

1. The bench was as cold as ice. ----------------------

2. This cafeteria is a zoo. ----------------------

3. Janice and Lin are two peas in a pod. ----------------------

4. His eyes sparkled like sunlit water. ----------------------

5. Life is a highway. ----------------------

6. We were packed in the elevator like sardines in a can. ----------------------

EXERCISE 3

What type of figurative language is used in each sentence? Write your answer on the line.

1. The ice cream sundae was calling her name.   _____

2. It took the might of Hercules, but Will moved the mattress all on his own.   _____

3. It's so hot you could fry an egg on the sidewalk!   _____

4. The smell of freshly baked bread greeted us at the door.   _____

5. After a long day of hiking, the campers hit the sack.   _____

6. My friend's bakery burned down last night. Now his business is toast.   _____

7. This suitcase weighs a ton!   _____

8. The bacon sizzled in the cast-iron skillet.   _____

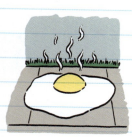

EXERCISE 4

Use personification to finish the sentences below. If you get stuck, borrow a vivid verb from the word bank.

> played   comforted   winked   shared   wheezed   welcomed
> embraced   revealed   teased   captured   danced   cried out   wept
> transported   chose   stared   marched   beckoned   rallied   protested
> whined   lifted   fought   taunted   cradled   rocked   threatened   waved

1. The stream

2. The stars

3. The breeze

4. The shoes

5. The train

EXERCISE 5

Use onomatopoeia to finish the sentences below.

1. The bottle

2. My stomach

3. The snake

4. The gravel

BONUS! Use onomatopoeia in a sentence of your own!

EXERCISE 6

Rewrite each sentence to add hyperbole.

1. My room is messy.

2. Mike's head hurt from studying.

3. Ike got taller this year.

4. The car trip was long.

5. Piper felt hot at the beach.

Read the excerpt from Gary Soto's short story "The Bike." Respond to the questions below.

> My first bike got me nowhere, though the shadow I cast as I pedaled raced along my side. The leaves of bird-filled trees stirred a warm breeze and litter scuttled out of the way. Our orange cats looked on from the fence, their tails up like antennas. I opened my mouth, and wind tickled the back of my throat.

1. Find all the uses of personification in the excerpt. (Hint! There are four.)

2. What kind of figurative language is "scuttled" an example of?

3. Find a simile in the excerpt.

4. Pick a sentence and rewrite it to add hyperbole.

5. Describe how Soto uses figurative language to create vivid sensory imagery.

EXERCISE 8

Underline the **IDIOM** in each sentence. Then use context clues to rewrite the sentence, translating figurative language into literal language.

1. Her friends were nervous for the final exam, but Gabby was cool as a cucumber.

2. When her speech received a standing ovation, Akilah knew the election was in the bag.

3. The students were in hot water after the principal found graffiti on her office wall.

4. A good mechanic would never cut corners.

5. There's no pop quiz—I'm just pulling your leg.

6. To break the ice, Marnie suggested playing two truths and a lie.

EXERCISE 9

Make a pun by matching each joke to its punchline.

1. What did the cat say after getting bad news? _____

2. Why shouldn't you use a broken pencil? _____

3. What happens if you steal coffee? _____

4. How did the lumberjack sleep? _____

5. What did the painting say in jail? _____

6. Why did Emily ace the math quiz? _____

7. Where do baby fish sleep? _____

8. Why was the elf hoarding candy canes? _____

A. They were in mint condition.

B. I was framed!

C. Like a log.

D. It was easy as pi.

E. You get grounded.

F. It is pointless.

G. You've got to be kitten me.

H. In bass-in-nets

EXERCISE 10

Write a sentence using each type of allusion: religious, literary, mythological, **and** historical.

1. Religious allusion

2. Literary allusion

3. Mythological allusion

4. Historical allusion

BONUS EXERCISE!

Look up the lyrics to your favorite song, and go on a figurative language scavenger hunt!

Song name:

Artist:

1. Try to find one example of each kind of figurative language in the lyrics:

   ▶ Idiom

   > But don't worry if you can't find one of each!

   ▶ Metaphor

   ▶ Simile

   ▶ Personification

   ▶ Allusion

▶ Hyperbole

▶ Pun

▶ Onomatopoeia

2. What kind of figurative language did this artist use the most?

3. What is your favorite lyric in the song? Does it use any kind of figurative language?

4. How does the figurative language affect your listening experience?

10 WORD CHOICE " „ !

WORD CHOICE refers to the decisions a writer makes when choosing which words to use.

Words with similar definitions can have subtle differences in meaning. Choosing the best words helps a writer achieve their **PURPOSE**.

PURPOSE
A writer's reason for writing. Maybe they want to write a scary story that will frighten the reader. Maybe they are writing an expository essay to educate readers on screaming hairy armadillos!

DENOTATION is a word's literal meaning—that is, the definition you'll get when you look it up in the dictionary. Words with similar denotations are called **SYNONYMS**.

CONNOTATION is the idea or feeling a word creates when it is used. Words with the same denotation can have different connotations.

THINK:
Understanding connotation can help you choose words that create a mood or evoke specific feelings in your writing.

Understanding the denotations and connotations of words helps writers improve their word choice and strengthen their writing.

Examples:

From the window, the children see their teacher getting into his car.

The connotation feels positive; it implies that the students are being respectful.

From the window, the children spy their teacher getting into his car.

The connotation feels negative; it implies that the students might be sneaky or intrusive.

The words "see" and "spy" have the same denotation— to perceive something with your eyes. But they have different connotations. Changing the word "see" to "spy" changes the feeling of the sentence.

Examples:

Pleasant!
Breathe in!

The fragrance from the kitchen wafted through the house.

UGGGH! Unpleasant!
Hold your nose!

The odor from the kitchen wafted through the house.

"Odor" and "fragrance" have the same denotation—a specific smell or scent. But they have different connotations. Replacing the word "smell" with "fragrance" or "odor" changes the feeling of the sentence.

EXERCISE 1

Compare the teal words in each set of sentences. Do they have different **DENOTATIONS** or different **CONNOTATIONS?** State your answer for each.

If they have different connotations, describe how the meaning of the sentence is changed by word choice.

1. ----------------------

Over the summer, we rented a hut by the lake.

Over the summer, we rented a chalet by the lake.

2. ----------------------

Monica packed her backpack with all the essentials she needed for camp.

Monica crammed her backpack with all the essentials she needed for camp.

153

3. ----------------------

The furniture we found in Abuela's garage was old.

The furniture we found in Abuela's garage was vintage.

4. ----------------------

After the buffet, Kiera was ravenous.

After the buffet, Kiera was stuffed.

5. ----------------------

The team chatted in the locker room.

The team gossiped in the locker room.

6. ----------------------

Tommy is very picky when it comes to cheese.

Tommy is very selective when it comes to cheese.

7. ----------------------

The older kids comforted Jim when he fell out of the window.

The older kids ridiculed Jim when he fell out of the window.

8. ----------------------

The boat swayed in the water.

The boat lurched in the water.

EXERCISE 2

Match each word with a negative connotation to its synonym with a positive connotation.

1. Smirk _____   A. Overripe

2. Brainwash _____   B. Confident

3. Babble _____   C. Persuade

4. Decrepit _____   D. Smile

5. Frugal _____   E. Search

6. Rotten _____   F. Thrifty

7. Arrogant _____   G. Talk

8. Snoop _____   H. Old

Pick a pair of words. Write one sentence for each word to demonstrate the difference in their connotations.

EXERCISE 3

Replace the teal word in each sentence with a synonym that has a slightly different connotation. Then describe how the synonym you chose changes the meaning of the sentence.

EXAMPLE:

Kim's room is neat.

Kim's room is *immaculate*.

Both words mean clean, but "neat" implies a general tidiness, while "immaculate" implies perfection.

1. The neighbor was curious.

   The neighbor was _____.

2. The group sat together at lunch.

   The _____ sat together at lunch.

3. Brian's parents are strict.

    Brian's parents are _____.

4. Marisa can be very pushy.

    Marisa can be very _____.

5. The music was playing so loud we didn't hear the fire alarm.

    The music was _____ so loud we didn't hear the fire alarm.

6. Ba rolled down the windows because the car was warm.

Ba rolled down the windows because the car was _____.

EXERCISE 4

Read the excerpt from Amy Tan's essay "Fish Cheeks." Consider the way Tan's word choice reveals the narrator's feelings. Then answer the questions.

When I found out that my parents had invited the minister's family over for Christmas Eve dinner, I cried. What would Robert think of our shabby Chinese Christmas? What would he think of our noisy Chinese relatives who lacked proper American manners? What terrible disappointment would he feel upon seeing not a roasted turkey and sweet potatoes but Chinese food?

On Christmas Eve I saw that my mother had outdone herself in creating a strange menu. She was pulling black veins out of the backs of fleshy prawns. The kitchen was littered with appalling mounds of raw food: A slimy rock cod with bulging fish eyes that pleaded not to be thrown into a pan of hot oil. Tofu, which looked like stacked wedges of rubbery white sponges. A bowl soaking dried fungus back to life.

1. How do you think the narrator feels about the minister's family coming to Christmas Eve dinner at their house?

2. How does Tan's word choice reveal the narrator's feelings? Identify at least two examples of her word choice and explain how their denotation or connotation affects the tone of the passage.

3. Read paragraph one. Circle the words and phrases with negative denotations or connotations.

4. Pretend the narrator is excited to have the minister's family over for dinner. Rewrite paragraph one, replacing the words you identified in question three with words and phrases that have a positive connotation.

5. Read paragraph two. Circle the words and phrases with negative denotations or connotations.

6. Pretend the narrator thinks the Christmas Eve meal looks delicious! Replace the words you circled in question four with words that make the food sound delectable!

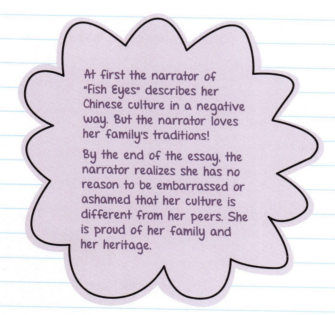

At first the narrator of "Fish Eyes" describes her Chinese culture in a negative way. But the narrator loves her family's traditions!

By the end of the essay, the narrator realizes she has no reason to be embarrassed or ashamed that her culture is different from her peers. She is proud of her family and her heritage.

EXERCISE 5

Your sister hurt her friend's feelings and she wants to send an apology text. She needs your help! Use what you know about word choice to fill in the blanks with the perfect words, to help your sister make amends.

Alison, I feel _____ about what

happened at school earlier today. I didn't mean

to _____ you in front of everyone. I

shouldn't have _____ the story you

_____ with me in _____.

It was bad enough that you _____ out

of the bathroom without _____ the

toilet paper _____ to your shoe. It was

_____ of me to _____ it to

the whole class! I'll never forget the _____

on your face when the students _____.

I know you are probably _____ with me.

Can you ever _____ me?

EXERCISE 6

Consider the impact that word choice makes in each sentence. Replace the teal word with a new word that makes the sentence stronger.

Feel free to change more than one word or rewrite the sentence to make your word choice work!

1. Jack went across the finish line and won his first race.

2. Brandi angrily took the diary from her snooping sister.

3. "Don't touch the hot stove, Mateo!" the babysitter said.

4. Mae lifted the weak necklace from the box and carefully tried it on.

5. Going up the craggy cliffside was exciting!

6. Mason took the heavy buckets of rocks to the garden.

7. After hours of turbulence, the passengers were pleased the plane landed safely.

8. When the tiger left its cage, the acrobats began to scream!

165

Chapter 11 TONE

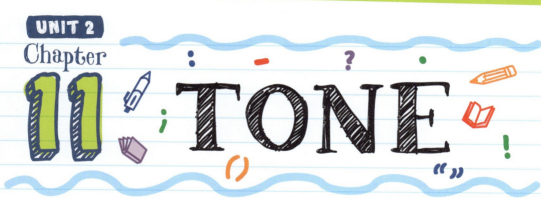

TONE is the attitude words convey. Throughout a piece of writing, the tone can change, or it can stay the same.

TONE WORDS

There are hundreds of tone words, but here are some good ones to know:

FORMAL Respectful, clear, concise, factual

INFORMAL Casual, conversational

PESSIMISTIC Negative, despairing, doubtful

OPTIMISTIC Positive, hopeful, cheerful

CONTEMPLATIVE Reflective, introspective, thoughtful

PLAYFUL Happy, carefree, lighthearted, silly

SERIOUS Solemn, earnest, business-like

INSPIRATIONAL Encouraging, reassuring, motivating

NOSTALGIC Wistful, sentimental, thinking about the past

CRITICAL Finding fault, disapproving, judgmental

PERSUASIVE Convincing, passionate, influential

Writers use **LITERARY DEVICES** to establish tone.

> **LITERARY DEVICE**
> a technique that makes writing interesting and unique

WORD CHOICE is a literary device. It affects tone because denotations and connotations cause different reactions in a reader.

Examples:

creates an excited, engaged tone

Sara's eyes <u>gleamed</u> as the fireworks <u>erupted</u> above her.

creates a bored, disengaged tone

Sara's eyes <u>glazed over</u> as the fireworks <u>went off</u> above her.

FIGURATIVE LANGUAGE is a literary device. It affects tone because it creates images that can generate different emotions and reactions in a reader.

Examples:

Love is the rosy cloud in the morning of life. —*Washington Irving*

Love is a hawk with velvet claws. —*Kurt Vonnegut*

Love is a disease. —*Ivan Turgenev*

THINK:
Each of these metaphors is about love, but they communicate very different feelings. How does each create a different tone?

REPETITION repeats a word or phrase over and over again to emphasize an idea, or play with tempo and rhythm.

Example:

Martin Luther King Jr. used repetition in his "I Have a Dream" speech to create an inspiring, determined tone.

We can never be satisfied as long as our bodies, heavy with the fatigue of travel, cannot gain lodging in the motels of the highways and the hotels of the cities.

We can never be satisfied as long as our children are stripped of their selfhood and robbed of their dignity by signs stating "for whites only."

ALLITERATION is when two or more words start with the same sound. It's a type of repetition!

Examples:

creates a light, energetic tone

The tiny turtledoves twittered and tweeted in the trees!

The dreary dog drooped with disappointment.

creates a heavy, tedious tone

RHYME is a literary device that repeats similar sounds in different words, especially at the end of lines. Like repetition, rhyme influences the rhythm and energy of writing, which can affect the tone.

Example:

In his poem "Stopping by Woods on a Snowy Evening," Robert Frost uses rhyme to create a tranquil, contemplative tone and convey the feeling of being in a snowy forest after dark.

The words all end in -eep!

The woods are lovely dark and <u>deep</u>,
But I have promises to <u>keep</u>,
And miles to go before I <u>sleep</u>,
And miles to go before I <u>sleep</u>.

Hey, this looks like repetition!

EXERCISE 1

Match each sentence about starting school with the word that best describes its tone.

1. School starts on Monday. _____

2. I don't think school starts on Monday. _____

3. Really? How could you not know that school starts on Monday? _____

4. Why does summer vacation have to be over? I don't want school to start again! _____

5. School is starting and I know it's going to be a great year! _____

6. School starts on Monday, so I already have my clothes picked out and my backpack packed! _____

7. Do you remember how fun the first day of school was last year? _____

8. I don't want to go to school on Monday. It's probably going to be a stressful year. _____

A. Whiny

B. Optimistic

C. Sentimental

D. Condescending

E. Objective

F. Anxious

G. Excited

H. Doubtful

EXERCISE 2

It's your turn! Write a sentence that demonstrates each tone. Use literary devices like figurative language, word choice, repetition, rhyme, or alliteration.

1. Stubborn

2. Persuasive

3. Resigned

4. Sincere

5. Mocking

6. Outraged

7. Nostalgic

8. Impartial

EXERCISE 3

Replace the teal word in each sentence below with a word that changes the tone of the sentence. Write the tone of each sentence on the lines. The first is done for you.

1. Molly skipped down the hallway to math class.   _____Cheerful_____

   Molly *trudged* down the hallway to math class.   _____Dreary_____

2. The nurse gave me a strained smile.   _____

   The nurse gave me a _____ smile.   _____

3. Corey weaved his way through the crowd.   _____

   Corey _____ his way through
   the crowd.   _____

4. Georgia was concerned about her grades.   _____

   Georgia was _____ about her grades.   _____

5. I chuckled as the muddy toddlers waddled through the kitchen.   _____

I _____ as the muddy toddlers waddled through the kitchen.   _____

6. Marcus smiled at his younger brother.   _____

Marcus _____ at his younger brother.   _____

7. The audience howled at the comedian's joke.   _____

The audience _____ at the comedian's joke.   _____

8. Lincoln snatched the money from his friend's wallet.   _____

Lincoln _____ the money from his friend's wallet.   _____

EXERCISE 4

Read the opening passage to John Steinbeck's novella *Of Mice and Men.* Identify the tone and underline the WORDS and PHRASES that help create the tone.

A FEW MILES south of Soledad, the Salinas River drops in close to the hillside bank and runs deep and green. The water is warm too, for it has slipped twinkling over the yellow sands in the sunlight before reaching the narrow pool. On one side of the river the golden foothill slopes curve up to the strong and rocky Gabilan mountains, but on the valley side the water is lined with trees—willows fresh and green with every spring, carrying in their lower leaf junctures the debris of the winter's flooding; and sycamores with mottled, white, recumbent limbs and branches that arch over the pool. On the sandy bank under the trees the leaves lie deep and so crisp that a lizard makes a great skittering if he runs among them. Rabbits come out of the brush to sit on the sand in the evening, and the damp flats are covered with the night tracks of 'coons, and with the spread pads of dogs from the ranches, and with the split-wedge tracks of deer that come to drink in the dark.

The tone of this passage is _____.

EXERCISE 5

Imagine John Steinbeck wanted to convey a different tone. Pick one of the passages below and replace words and phrases to create an eerie, ominous tone.

1. "A few miles south of Soledad, the Salinas River drops in close to the hillside bank and runs deep and green. The water is warm too, for it has slipped twinkling over the yellow sands in the sunlight before reaching the narrow pool."

2. "On one side of the river the golden foothill slopes curve up to the strong and rocky Gabilan mountains, but on the valley side the water is lined with trees—willows fresh and green with every spring, carrying in their lower leaf junctures the debris of the winter's flooding; and sycamores with mottled, white, recumbent limbs and branches that arch over the pool."

EXERCISE 6

Read Langston Hughes's poem "Dreams" and respond to the questions below.

Dreams

Hold fast* to dreams
For if dreams die
Life is a broken-winged bird
That cannot fly.

Hold fast to dreams
For when dreams go
Life is a barren field
Frozen with snow.

*Here, "fast" means "tight"!

Langston Hughes was a twentieth-century novelist, poet, and playwright and was a leader of the Harlem Renaissance. His writing celebrated African American culture and condemned racial injustice.

1. How do you feel after reading the poem?

2. What is the message of the poem?

3. What word would you use to describe the tone of this poem? Circle four words or phrases that capture the tone.

4. Does the tone of the poem change or stay the same? Support your answer with examples.

5. Find a metaphor in the poem. How does the metaphor help establish the tone?

6. Underline examples of repetition in the poem. How does repetition affect the tone?

Chapter 12: TEXTUAL ANALYSIS

TEXTUAL ANALYSIS is the close study of a **TEXT**. You can use textual analysis in a short response or an essay to understand, discuss, or interpret a specific element of a text.

> A text can be any original work, not just a book or short story.

Textual analysis can help you study a character in a book, the theme of a song, imagery in a poem, figurative language in a speech, symbolism in a painting, the tone of a film, the marketing strategies in a commercial, data in a graph, irony in a political cartoon, or word choice in a letter or email.

How to analyze a text:

1. Study the text. Read (or watch, or experience) the entire text and think about important themes, the author's purpose, and other elements that stand out.

2. Decide what you want to analyze. It could be anything—the setting, tone, character development, use of figurative language, or narration style. Whatever element you choose, it should be interesting and relevant to the meaning of the text.

Example:

Your teacher tells you to analyze how Ray Bradbury establishes tone in his short story "All Summer in a Day."

3. Establish your **CENTRAL IDEA**. This is what you are saying about the part of the text you are analyzing. Think of it as your argument or your point.

central idea

Example:

In "All Summer in a Day," Ray Bradbury's word choice and use of figurative language to describe the setting create a melancholy tone.

CENTRAL IDEA

Central idea is the author's message about the topic. Some teachers call this the main idea, controlling idea, topic sentence, or thesis statement.

4. Find **EVIDENCE** in the text to support your central idea. Evidence is information, facts, **QUOTATIONS**, observations, or examples that prove our point. It can be **EXPLICIT** or **IMPLICIT**.

EXPLICIT EVIDENCE is stated directly in the text. The reader doesn't have to make an **INFERENCE** to see how explicit evidence supports the central idea.

> **INFERENCE**
> a conclusion based on evidence in the text

Example:

directly states that it rained constantly

"It had been raining for seven years; thousands upon thousands of days compounded and filled from one end to the other with rain . . ."

QUOTATION
the repetition of the exact language a writer used, set in quotation marks

monotonous word choice directly creates a dismal mood

IMPLICIT EVIDENCE is not stated directly in the text, but the reader can use context to infer how it supports the central idea.

Example:

"[Margot] was a very frail girl who looked as if she had been lost in the rain for years and the rain had washed out the blue from her eyes and the red from her mouth and the yellow from her hair."

This passage doesn't directly describe the weather but it uses figurative language to imply the rain makes Margot sad.

THINK:

A text will be full of information related to your central idea, but not all of that information will prove your point. Only use information that directly supports your central idea as evidence.

This doesn't support the central idea. It doesn't show how the rainy setting makes the "rocket" people sad.

✗ "Rocket men and women" created a civilization on Venus, where it never stops raining.

✓ Margot's classmate begins to cry when she feels a raindrop hit her palm, after an hour of running around in the sunlight.

This supports the central idea because it shows that the rain made Margot's classmate sad.

5. Put it all together! Usually, your textual analysis will be in the form of a written response, like a paragraph or an essay. It might be helpful to start with a summary of the text, so your reader has context for your analysis.

A **SUMMARY** is a shortened retelling of something. Summaries **PARAPHRASE** a writer's original language and only include details and facts that get the main point of the text across.

PARAPHRASE
to put something someone else has said or written into your own words

Example:

[The children] ran among the trees, they slipped and fell, they pushed each other, they played hide-and-seek and tag, but most of all they squinted at the sun until the tears ran down their faces; they put their hands up to that yellowness and that amazing blueness and they breathed of the fresh, fresh air and listened and listened to the silence which suspended them in a blessed sea of no sound and no motion. They looked at everything and savored everything. Then, wildly, like animals escaped from their caves, they ran and ran in shouting circles. They ran for an hour and did not stop running.

SUMMARY:
When the rain stopped, the children played games in the sunshine for an hour. They observed how warm and bright the sun was, and how quiet and fresh it was outside, without rain.

An **OBJECTIVE SUMMARY** does not include your personal opinions or judgments about a text. This is the best kind of summary to use for textual analysis.

Example:

▶ Objective summary of "All Summer in a Day":

"All Summer in a Day" takes place on Venus, where it rains constantly, and the sun shines for only one hour every seven years. On the day the sun is going to shine, Margot's classmates lock her in a closet and forget about her when the sun comes out. They play in the sunshine, and when the rain starts again they remember Margot is still locked in the closet. They feel guilty and let her out.

A **SUBJECTIVE SUMMARY** includes personal opinions, interpretations, or emotions. You should NOT use subjective summary for textual analysis. You might use it if you are writing a personal response paragraph, where you need to share your opinions or reflect on your feelings.

Example:

▶ Subjective summary of "All Summer in a Day":

opinion

This interesting story takes place on Venus, where it rains *opinion* way too much, and the sun only shines once every seven years. When the sun comes out, Margot's mean classmates lock her in a closet, and it is so sad! *personal feeling* They forget about her as they play in the sun. Then, when the rain starts again, they let her out. I think they are very rude, and Margot should have been able to play in the sun too.

opinion that reflects on the story, instead of describing the events

Use **FINS** to check if your summary is objective:

Fact-check: Check what you've written against what you've just read.

Important details only: Include only the main details and facts.

No opinions: Stick to the facts so your summary is objective.

Sequence your details: The order of events and information in your summary should usually match the order in which they appear in the text.

EXERCISE 1

Match each term to the correct definition.

1. Textual analysis _____

2. Inference _____

3. Implicit evidence _____

4. Explicit evidence _____

5. Objective summary _____

6. Paraphrase _____

7. Quotation _____

8. Evidence _____

9. Central idea _____

A. Putting original writing into your own words

B. A conclusion based on evidence and context

C. Details that support a central idea and are understood through context

D. Repeating words or a passage from a text exactly

E. The close study of a text to uncover the author's deeper meaning

F. Facts and information from a text

G. Details that support the central idea and that are clearly stated in a text

H. The point you are making with textual analysis

I. A recap that does not include personal opinions

EXERCISE 2

Perfect your paraphrasing skills by practicing on the passages below.

Psst! Just put them in your own words! And remember, you don't need to include every detail, just the important ones.

1. "The fable writer Aesop, who lived c. 620–560 BCE, was most likely an Ethiopian. He brought animist tales to the wider world when he was enslaved and taken to Greece as the property of a man named Iadmon. For the rest of his life Aesop lived on the island of Samos, Greece, just north of the Mediterranean on the Aegean Sea. . . . It's unclear just when or how he was able to gain his freedom, but the story traditions he brought with him from Africa were likely his path out of bondage."

—*African Icons*, by Tracey Baptiste

2 "Even the hardest, oldest glacial ice isn't solid like a rock. It's filled with tiny air bubbles, like a piece of bread. This air is then buried deeper and deeper in the glacier as time passes and snow packs on top of it. Air bubbles have been buried in the oldest glaciers for millennia, and they are like time capsules—tiny breaths of air from past eons."

—*Meltdown*, by Anita Sanchez

3 "Ghost lights are mysterious orbs of light that appear over bogs and marshes. Also known as will-o'-the-wisps, they are thought to be mischievous spirits of the dead that try to lead travelers into dangerous areas. Some scientists have another explanation: They say the flickering lights could be swamp gases catching fire."

—*Frightlopedia*, by Julie Winterbottom

4 "Mary Shelley is one of the youngest writers ever to produce a genuine classic. She was only eighteen when she wrote *Frankenstein*.

"The story came to her while she was on vacation in Switzerland with her future husband, Percy Shelley, and their friends Lord Byron and Dr. John Polidori. The group was trapped in a Swiss château by bad weather, bored out of their skulls. Byron suggested that they each write a scary story to read to the group. When Mary chose to write about someone who tried to create life and instead created a murderous monster who eventually did him in, she may have been thinking about her own mother, the great feminist writer Mary Wollstonecraft, who was indeed killed by her own creation: She died giving birth to Mary Shelley."

—*The Big Book of Monsters*, by Hal Johnson

EXERCISE 3

Pretend you are writing an essay analyzing Isaac Asimov's short story "The Fun They Had." Your central idea is that the story takes place in the future. Read the passage below and highlight examples of explicit evidence and implicit evidence that support this central idea.

Margie even wrote about it that night in her diary. On the page headed May 17, 2155, she wrote, "Today Tommy found a real book!"

It was a very old book. Margie's grandfather once said that when he was a little boy *his* grandfather told him that there was a time when all stories were printed on paper. . . .

"Gee," said Tommy, "what a waste. When you're through with the book, you just throw it away, I guess. Our television screen must have had a million books on it and it's good for plenty more. I wouldn't throw it away."

"Same with mine," said Margie. She was eleven and hadn't seen as many telebooks as Tommy had.

1. Give one example of explicit evidence that this story takes place in the future:

2. Give one example of implicit evidence that this story takes place in the future:

3. Did you find more explicit evidence or more implicit evidence in the passage? Why do you think that might be?

In Asimov's story, the teachers are machines, not humans! Is that evidence the story takes place in the future?

Read the excerpt from Jasmine Warga's novel *Other Words for Home* about a 12-year-old refugee named Jude whose family moves to Ohio to escape the Syrian civil war.

In America,
it seems like everyone has money,
new shiny sneakers
bright-colored lipstick
pants that fit just right.

Then I start to notice the man on the corner
with a sign begging people for help,
the tired woman waiting for the bus
with shoes that are cracked at the sole.

America, I realize,
has its sad and tired
parts too.

America,
like every other place in the world,
is a place where some people sleep
and some people
other people
dream.

Write a short response paragraph that analyzes Jude's perception of America:

> ▶ Come up with a central idea.
>
> ▶ Underline at least two pieces of evidence that support your central idea.
>
> ▶ Use your central idea and evidence to write a short response paragraph.

Central idea:

EXERCISE 5

Read the news article below. Write an objective summary of the article in a short paragraph.

Sixth-Grader Wins Spelling Bee

BY KELLY SCARDINA

On Monday, May 1, 2023, after three hours of competition, Joshua Ninmann became the first sixth-grader to win the Herricks Middle School annual spelling bee. With more than 100 students participating from grades six through eight, Ninmann became the winning contestant when he correctly spelled the word *insouciant*, meaning exhibiting or characterized by freedom from concern or care.

Ninmann, a new student to the district, moved to Herricks over the summer. He started middle school in the district in September and has made the honor roll all three quarters during the 2022–2023 school year. With a GPA of 4.0, Ninmann is also a member of the mathletes club and class treasurer for his grade. He won first place in the science fair in February and recently had a short story published in *Teen Ink* magazine.

"Joshua is one of the most passionate readers in my class," says Gina Glanzman, sixth grade Language Arts Teacher. "Children who are avid readers and who show skills in writing and reading comprehension usually do well."

Ninmann says he used various ways to prepare for the bee. "I went beyond just memorizing lists of spelling words. I also spent time learning root words, so I could see similar patterns in words and spell them correctly."

Ninmann will go on to compete in the Nassau County Spelling Bee this June. More than 200 middle school students will compete at C. W. Post Community College. The winner will go on to the Scripps National Spelling Bee with the opportunity to win a trophy and over $52,000 in prize money.

"I hope to make it to the final round," says Ninmann. With dreams of attending Yale one day, Ninmann states, "The money would help pay for college."

EXERCISE 6

Read this summary of the novel *Okay for Now*, by Gary D. Schmidt, that an eighth-grader included in a textual analysis paper. Underline where the summary is subjective. Then rewrite the summary so it is objective.

In *Okay for Now*, the main character, Doug Sweiteck, has a terrible life! His father is an abusive alcoholic who hits his kids, bullies his wife, and loses one job after another. Doug's father is a miserable man. I think Doug's brothers learned to be abusive from their dad because they are also mean. They follow in their father's footsteps, tormenting Doug by hitting him and bullying him. This is despicable behavior, in my opinion. When Doug receives a signed cap from Joe Pepitone of the New York Yankees, his older brother takes it and passes it around school until it ends up in a rainy gutter. I would be furious if my brother stole something special from me. What's worse is that his father has also lost his job, and so the whole family has to pick up and move to Marysville. Doug is sad he won't be able to attend eighth grade at Camillo Jr. High with his friends. When Doug's family is packing the car to move, his very kind best friend Holling Hoodhood lifts Doug's spirits by giving him Joe Pepitone's signed jacket as a moving away gift. It was such a thoughtful gesture. I would feel so much better if someone did that for me. This shows the theme of the book: good friends can help you cope with the hardships you face.

EXERCISE 7

Analyze your favorite television show (or your favorite movie or your favorite book). Come up with a central idea and use textual evidence and a summary to develop your idea.

Central idea:

Unit 3

WRITING

Writing is one of the most important skills you can develop. Let's practice some of the most common forms of writing you'll encounter in middle school: narratives, arguments, informative texts, and explanatory texts.

Chapter 13 ? WRITING NARRATIVES !

NARRATIVE WRITING is writing that tells a story.

In a **FICTIONAL** narrative, the author creates a story from their imagination.

In a **NONFICTION** narrative, the writer tells a true story about real events, their life, or the lives of others.

A **NARRATOR** is the person or entity telling the story. **SUBJECTIVE NARRATORS** reveal the thoughts and feelings of a character. **OBJECTIVE NARRATORS** describe a character's behavior and dialogue but not their thoughts and feelings.

? UNRELIABLE NARRATORS

Narrators can be RELIABLE or UNRELIABLE. A reliable narrator has a perspective that accurately describes the events and details of the story. An unreliable narrator has a perspective that does not accurately describe the events and details, so the reader might not be able to trust them. A narrator might be unreliable because of age, attitude, or psychological state.

often abbreviated to POV!

POINT OF VIEW is the perspective a narrator tells the story from. There are three points of view in narrative writing.

FIRST-PERSON POV	SECOND-PERSON POV	THIRD-PERSON POV
▶ Narrator is a character in the story	▶ Narrator addresses the reader directly, as if the reader is a character	▶ Narrator is an outsider looking in, not a character in the story
▶ Uses pronouns like "I," "me," "my," "we," and "ours"	▶ Uses the pronouns "you" and "yours"	▶ Uses the pronouns "he," "she," and "they"
▶ Is SUBJECTIVE	▶ Is SUBJECTIVE	▶ Can be SUBJECTIVE or OBJECTIVE
▶ The reader knows only what that narrator knows.	▶ Helps the reader relate to the story.	▶ The narrator may reveal the thoughts and feelings of multiple characters or stick to just one character.

Example:

The novel *To Kill a Mockingbird*, by Harper Lee, is written in first-person point of view. The main character, Scout Finch, is the narrator. This is the novel's opening sentence:

"When he was nearly thirteen, my brother Jem got his arm badly broken at the elbow."

← This pronoun shows that the narrator is using 1st-person POV!

In second-person POV, this sentence would be:

"When he was nearly thirteen, your brother Jem got his arm badly broken at the elbow."

2nd-person pronoun!

In third-person POV, it would be:

"When he was nearly thirteen, Scout's brother Jem got his arm badly broken at the elbow."

3rd person!

SETTING is where and when a narrative takes place.

Writers establish the setting with details: sounds, sights, smells, and textures of a place. Sometimes writers reference historical events to establish time period and location.

Example:

To Kill a Mockingbird is set in Maycomb, Alabama, in the 1930s.

In rainy weather the streets turned to red slop; grass grew on the sidewalks, the courthouse sagged in the square. . . . But it was a time of vague optimism for some of the people: Maycomb County had recently been told that it had nothing to fear but fear itself.

Southern Alabama has red dirt, and in the 1930s, rural roads were not paved.

This is a reference to a speech made by President Franklin D. Roosevelt during the Great Depression.

CHARACTERS are the actors in a narrative who carry out the plot. Strong characters have interesting **CHARACTERISTICS** that readers learn as the story unfolds.

Characters learn and grow throughout a story in a process called **CHARACTER DEVELOPMENT**.

CHARACTERISTICS
details about the way a character looks, sounds, and behaves; what is important to them; and what they believe

Example:

In *To Kill a Mockingbird*, Scout is the main character, and her neighbor Boo Radley is a supporting character. At the beginning of the story, Boo Radley is a mysterious figure who never leaves his house and is feared by the neighborhood kids. *characteristics* By the end, Boo is revealed to be a kind neighbor when he overcomes his fear of leaving his house and saves Scout from being attacked. *character development*

PLOT is the sequence of events in a story.

Plots usually have a central **CONFLICT** that moves the story forward, and causes characters to develop.

Example:

plot { *To Kill a Mockingbird* is a coming-of-age story set in a segregated Alabama town. Scout lives with her father, Atticus Finch, and her older brother, Jem, and witnesses the consequences of racism when Atticus, a lawyer, defends Tom Robinson, a Black man accused of a crime he didn't commit. Scout's story begins when a boy named

plot { Dill comes to spend the summer with his aunt, who is Scout and Jem's neighbor, and the three kids plot to make Boo Radley, a town recluse, come out of his house.

← conflict

The **CONCLUSION** is the closing event of the plot, where conflicts are resolved, characters complete their development, and readers learn a lesson.

Example:

conflict is resolved → character development complete

In the conclusion of *To Kill a Mockingbird*, Scout finally meets Boo Radley and realizes her perception of him had been wrong all along. She learns that you shouldn't judge people based on rumors or stereotypes but on their actions and choices. } lesson learned!

Narrative Techniques

DIALOGUE is what characters say to each other. Effective dialogue conveys information, drives the story forward, and reveals a character's motivations. Dialogue is usually noted with quotation marks.

Example:

dialogue {
"I was—we were just tryin' to give somethin' to Mr. Radley." ← quotation marks

"What were you trying to give him?"

"Just a letter."

"Let me see it."

DESCRIPTIVE LANGUAGE helps a reader visualize the characters, setting, and events of a story. It includes figurative language, nuanced word choice, tone, and **SENSORY LANGUAGE**.

SENSORY LANGUAGE
describes how things look, sound, taste, smell, and feel

Example:

Harper Lee uses descriptive language to describe Boo Radley's spooky house:

sensory language →

The house was low, was once white with a deep front porch and green shutters, but had long ago darkened to the color of the slate-gray yard around it. Rain-rotted shingles drooped over the eaves of the veranda; oak trees kept the sun away. The remains of a picket drunkenly guarded the front yard.

↖ personification

EXERCISE 1

Read each passage and identify what point of view the narrator uses: first, second, or third.

1. It is the first day of school. You pull out your schedule and see that you're in Room 205 for first period. Carefully, you navigate your way through groups of middle schoolers moving rapidly in each direction. You try to avoid bumping into anyone as you make your way down the hall to Spanish class, weighed down by your heavy backpack and your violin case.

   Point of View: _____

2. "There's no way I am going to wear that!" I stubbornly insisted, holding the bright purple puffy coat as far away from my body as I could. I was in sixth grade, and I knew how to dress myself. The coat my grandmother picked out for me was not my style.

   Point of View: _____

3. Tamika was nervous. She knew she was fast, but all the other girls on the basketball court were a lot taller than her. She took three deep breaths to calm her nerves, and then sprang into action.

   Point of View: _____

4. You see them in the food court together. They told you they had to study, but now here they were eating French fries, sipping Cokes, and laughing together. Anger surges through your body. You wonder if you should confront them, show them that you know they lied to you, left you out again. Then, you feel tears prick the corners of your eyes. You run back to the parking lot, hoping you can still catch a ride home.

Point of View: _____

5. Syl was determined to start this year on a good note. They would go to all their classes, do all their assignments, and submit them on time too. They weren't going to procrastinate like last year. They weren't going to spend all their time playing Fortnite and putting their work to the side. It was a new beginning, and they had a clean slate.

Point of View: _____

EXERCISE 2

Now it's your turn! Write three paragraphs about a mysterious package. Write the first paragraph in first-person point of view, the second in second person, and the third in third person.

First-person point of view:

Second-person point of view:

Third-person point of view:

EXERCISE 3

Read each passage and use clues to determine the setting of the story. Underline the **CONTEXT CLUES** that helped you.

1. "Par ici," said the tour guide. The line to ascend the Eiffel Tower was long, longer than they expected. However, Gina was thrilled to see the city from so high. Ever since she read *Madeline* as a little girl, Gina had dreamed of visiting the City of Lights. In only forty minutes, she would emerge from the elevator and stand more than 1,000 feet above the sites she had visited just yesterday: the Basilica, the Louvre, and the Arc de Triomphe.

   Setting: _____

2. Brooke sat alone in the bleachers, watching the players scrimmage below. She knew it would be at least an hour before Kyle finished. This would be as good a time as any to revise the first draft of her essay for Mr. Kaplan's class tomorrow. She took one more glance at the team racing across the field and then reached into her backpack.

   Setting: _____

3. Quinn made his way up and down the aisles of the mystery section. He ran his fingers up and down the spines of the books, their covers carefully wrapped in plastic. He loved mystery and suspense novels, and his favorite author, Karen M. McManus, had finally released a new bestseller: *You'll Be the Death of Me*. It was time to start his summer reading, and he hoped the book would be waiting for him on the shelf, ready to be checked out.

   Setting: _____

4. It was dusk, and campers began to settle down around their tents. From her site, Lucy could hear the crackling of fires beginning to burn, twigs snapping slowly in the heat, and the occasional crunch of gravel as families moved around their sites, stringing wet bathing suits and towels on makeshift clotheslines and retrieving more firewood from the backs of their cars or the occasional drink from their coolers.

Setting: _____

5. "Houston, do you read me?" asked the commander anxiously. On the other end, she heard only static. "Houston, we have a problem," she repeated firmly into the radio. Her crew huddled around her on the quarterdeck as they listened in silence. Outside the window, they could still see Earth's surface, even if they couldn't generate a signal. That was a small comfort to the crew, as it had been ninety days since they had felt solid ground beneath their feet. The feeling of weightlessness was beginning to take its toll.

Setting: _____

EXERCISE 4

Come up with three settings. For each setting, write a paragraph that describes it with strong sensory language. Describe what you see, smell, taste, touch, hear, and feel in that setting. You can pick settings from the word bank or come up with your own!

street fair   bakery   farmer's market   alien's spaceship
set of your favorite TV show   boardwalk   an arcade

1. Setting: _____

REMEMBER:
A setting is where and when a story takes place. It can be specific (your childhood bedroom the night before your tenth birthday) or general (an open field at sunset).

2. Setting: _____

3. Setting: _____

EXERCISE 5

Circle whether each statement about narrative writing is TRUE or FALSE.

1. All narratives are fictional.   True   False

2. Narrative writing has a beginning, middle, and end.   True   False

3. Narrative writing explains how something works
   or how something is done.   True   False

4. Narrators are always reliable.   True   False

5. All narrators are objective and avoid showing
   their feelings or opinions.   True   False

6. Setting tells the reader the time and place of
   the story.   True   False

7. A third-person narrator uses the pronoun "I" when
   telling the story.   True   False

8. This line is subjective: The school library was a safe place
   for me during those first lonely weeks at my new school.   True   False

9. Narratives do not have a conflict.   True   False

10. Dialogue is what characters say to each other.   True   False

EXERCISE 6

Pick a novel or short story you have read recently. Use it to answer the questions below.

TITLE:

AUTHOR:

1. What is the setting of the story?

2. Who is the narrator?

3. What point of view does the narrator use to tell the story?

4. Summarize the plot.

5. What is the conflict in the story?

6. Who is your favorite character? Name three characteristics that make that character interesting.

7. Describe how that character developed or changed throughout the story.

8. Identify an effective example of dialogue in the text. What information is revealed through the dialogue? What does the dialogue reveal about the character?

9. What is the conclusion? Did it surprise you?

10. Find three examples of descriptive language used in the story.

EXERCISE 7

Read the fictional excerpts below. Add a line of dialogue to the narrative that shows the main character displaying the specified character trait.

EXAMPLE: Rude

Navi pushed her way through the crowded hallway. It was the first day of school, and she wasn't going to let a bunch of little sixth-graders slow her down and make her late to first period. As she headed down the corridor, a girl held out her schedule and began to ask her for directions to the gym. But it wasn't *her* job to help lost students. *"Move out of my way!" Navi yelled*.

1. Confident

It's the first day of school and I'm walking through the door with a whole new look. My hair is cropped short and dyed jet black, with a streak of green in the bangs. I'm wearing a distressed denim jacket I decorated with patches from my favorite bands and pins of my favorite book characters. My long blonde pigtails and frilly dresses are a thing of the past. I hear someone shout my name from across the hall, "Hunter, is that you? What happened?!"

2. Thoughtful

Demandre had finally finished shoveling his driveway. His hands were frozen, and his face was numb. He couldn't wait to get in the house, take off his snow pants and wet socks, and warm up. Then he saw his elderly neighbor, Mr. Stevens, attempting to shovel the heavy snow off his front stoop.

3. Heroic

You see the older boys teasing the new kid at his locker. You remember when you moved here a few years before how tough it was to make friends, fit in, and find a place where you belong. You know you can't walk past and pretend you don't see them pushing the new kid around. You walk toward them and their taunts grow louder.

4. Responsible

Cecilia opened her textbook. The earth science test was in a week. She wanted to be prepared. Science was her toughest subject, and she wanted to do her best. She had gone to a review session at the beginning of the week and allotted an hour each day to study. But just as Cecilia pulled out her index cards to study, her best friend walked up and invited her to go to the movies.

UNIT 3
Chapter
14 THE WRITING PROCESS

The **WRITING PROCESS** is a five-stage process that helps writers organize their ideas, make a plan, and create a strong, polished piece.

Stage 1. PREWRITING

Prewriting is when you organize your thoughts and ideas before you start to write. There are lots of things to do in this stage, so break it into steps:

STEP 1: Identify your **TASK**. What do you need to write?

Example:

Your English teacher gives you this essay prompt:
Examine a tradition or practice and evaluate whether it should continue or how it could change. } Your task is to write an essay evaluating a tradition.

STEP 2: **BRAINSTORM** topics to write about that fit the task. Then, pick your favorite one!

Example:

Possible Traditions
- Blowing out candles on a birthday cake
- Setting off fireworks on the Fourth of July
- Tossing coins into fountains
- Tipping at restaurants

STEP 3: What do you want to say about the topic you chose? Think about who your **AUDIENCE** is, and do some **RESEARCH** to learn more. It might help to do another brainstorm, this time focusing on your topic.

Example:

After doing reserach and brainstorming ideas, you decide you want to write about the hazards of fireworks and suggest alternative ways to celebrate the Fourth of July.

BRAINSTORMING TIP!

Set a timer for five minutes and write down everything you can think of that would fit the task. When the buzzer goes off, review your ideas, and highlight those that you think would best fit your task.

STEP 4: Establish your **CENTRAL IDEA**. A strong central idea is clear and specific and can be supported with evidence.

> **CENTRAL IDEA**
> one to two sentences that summarize what you are writing about and state your position clearly

Example:

Although fireworks are festive, and beautiful to watch, they are dangerous to use and harmful to the environment.

STEP 5: Create an **OUTLINE** that states what each paragraph will be about. Start the outline with your central idea, followed by supporting ideas and evidence. To complete the outline, you may need to do more research.

> **OUTLINE**
> a roadmap for your essay that organizes your ideas

> An outline doesn't need to be full of details or use complete sentences. It just needs to show what ideas you're going to put where.

Stage 2. DRAFTING

Use your outline to write a **FIRST DRAFT**.

> You will write a lot of drafts!

Each paragraph should include:

> **DRAFT**
> a rough version of a piece of writing

▶ a **TOPIC SENTENCE** that introduces a supporting idea

▶ **EVIDENCE** that supports the supporting idea

▶ **TRANSITION WORDS** that help readers move from one idea to the next

Example:

Here's a draft of a body paragraph:

transition words

In addition to the dangers they pose for humans, fireworks are harmful to the

transition words

environment. For example, fireworks create toxic gases that poison the air, water,

and soil. According to a study in the *International Journal of Environmental*

evidence

Research and Public Health, the pollution from Fourth of July fireworks is com-

evidence

transition words

parable to the pollution caused by big wildfires. In other words, the fun we

have on the Fourth of July has big consequences for our planet.   *topic sentence*

Don't worry about things like spelling and grammar in your first draft. Just keep writing! You'll make corrections in your later drafts through revision and editing.

Stage 3. REVISING

When you **REVISE**, you improve your first draft with changes to the content, organization, sentence structure, and word choice. You can revise the draft yourself, or you can ask a friend to **PEER REVIEW** it for you.

> When a peer looks over your work.

When revising, ask yourself these questions:

- Does the writing meet the guidelines for the assigned task?
- Is my central idea clear?
- Do I have at least two supporting ideas?
- Does each paragraph have a clear topic sentence?
- Did I include enough research, data, and text evidence to support my central and supporting ideas?
- Are my ideas arranged in a logical order?
- Are there transitions that help readers move from one idea to the next?
- Is my tone appropriate for my purpose and my audience?
- Is there anything I don't need to say that I can cut?

Then, use your notes and any feedback from your peers to write a **SECOND DRAFT**.

> You might revise multiple times and write multiple drafts before you are satisfied with the content and organization of your writing.

Stage 4. EDITING

When you are happy with the content, organization, and language of your writing, it's time to **EDIT**, fixing grammar, spelling, punctuation, and convention errors. Editing can include the following:

Editing is also called proofreading.

- Correcting capitalization
- Correcting punctuation
- Catching spelling errors
- Fixing run-on sentences, fragments, and comma splices
- Checking formatting font size, font type, and spacing

Rewrite your essay one more time to fix the errors you find. This draft is called your **FINAL DRAFT**.

Stage 5. PUBLISHING

The final stage of the writing process is **PUBLISHING** or sharing your final draft. In middle school, publishing might look like:

Turning in the final draft to a teacher

Posting on a blog

Sharing your work with friends and family

Submitting to a magazine, newspaper, or journal

Entering a writing competition

EXERCISE 1

Fill in each blank with a word from the word bank. You will use each word once.

> central idea   audience   task   prewriting
> first draft   publishing   editing   revising   outline

1. The planning stage before you begin to write   _____

2. Correcting spelling and grammar errors   _____

3. The people for whom you are writing   _____

4. A map of your essay that arranges your ideas and evidence   _____

5. Rearranging, adding, or removing paragraphs, sentences, or words to improve your draft   _____

6. What you are assigned to write   _____

7. Sharing your work with an audience   _____

8. A sentence or two that states the writer's position or opinion on the topic   _____

9. The initial version of a piece of writing   _____

EXERCISE 2

Read the passage below. Find the central idea. Find three pieces of supporting evidence. Find two transition words or phrases.

They might have tiny brains, but crows are one of the smartest animals on Earth. Scientists say that animals who use tools to complete tasks are intelligent. Crows use tools to hunt. And they don't just use the tools, they make the tools themselves, and teach each other how. They transform twigs into spears by stripping their leaves and carving hooks into the tip. Then they use these hooked spears to pull bugs and other critters from out of deep hiding spots. In addition, they can remember human faces they've seen just one time and will change their behavior toward a person if they recall behavior that was dangerous or extra kind. Furthermore, when a human feeds a crow, or does something kind to take care of it, crows have been known to bring the person an object as payment. This is called "gifting." Crows have gifted jewelry, keys, pretty rocks, and even money!

Jason is writing an article about his school's new backpack policy for the school newspaper. He emailed his principal to request an interview, but his tone is too informal. Revise Jason's email to give it a formal tone appropriate for communication with an administrator.

RE: Can u help?

Hey Mr. Hubbard,

I have this thing to write for our school newspaper. I heard you changed the backpack policy this year. Do we really have to put our backpacks in our lockers? Is this forreal? Tell me ur jokin. Some students are MAD about this new policy. They are fuming that they can't bring their backpacks to their classes now. If so, I'd like to ask you some questions about what changes you made and why. I am gonna use your interview to write the article up. I want to meet you this week to go over it. I'll come after school to get this done, and you tell me everything.

Peace out,
Jace

Send

EXERCISE 4

Read each scenario below and identify what stage of the writing process each student is in.

prewriting   outlining   drafting   revising   editing   publishing

1. Dottie is writing a narrative essay about her trip to Lake George for class. Looking back at her first draft, she would like to add more description about the sunset over the lake.

   What stage is Dottie in? _____

2. Donald's English teacher asked the class to write a sonnet. Donald knows the format of a sonnet, but he hasn't decided what he wants to write about yet.

   What stage is Donald in? _____

3. Phyllis is writing an editorial for her school newspaper about her school's new cell phone policy. She is not sure if her tone is appropriate. She would like her friend Marco to read it and give her feedback.

   What stage is Phyllis in? _____

4. Shanice has just finished reading five articles on plastic pollution for her research paper. She has many ideas but needs to organize them.

   What stage is Shanice in? _____

5. The editors of the school newspaper have finished revising and editing. They are sending the final drafts to the printer.

   What stage is the newspaper staff in? _____

6. Martin has completed his research essay outline and is ready to begin writing the paper.

   What stage is Martin in? _____

7. Kiera has been assigned to write a narrative about an experience that changed her. She needs to come up with a few ideas.

   What stage is Kiera in? _____

8. Cole's teacher gave him some feedback about his first draft of his poem. She suggested that he add more imagery. Cole is going to take her advice and work on his poem again.

   What stage is Cole in? _____

EXERCISE 5

Read the outline below. Answer the questions that follow.

Introduction: E-readers have revolutionized the literary world, but can readers give up traditional books for these electronic devices? Although some people might miss the smell and feel of the printed page, an e-reader offers a better reading experience than a print book.

Paragraph 2: E-readers are more portable than print books.
   a. E-readers don't take up much space.
   b. E-readers are lightweight.
   c. E-readers can hold hundreds of titles at once, meaning people can carry more books with them.

Paragraph 3: E-readers offer convenience that print books cannot.
   a. E-readers have a light, so readers can read in the dark.
   b. E-readers allow readers to adjust the font size and style.
   c. E-readers offer access to any title instantly.
   d. E-readers can access titles at lower prices.

Conclusion: Although many readers still prefer the old-fashioned print book and the sensory experiences that come with it, there is no denying that e-readers are the way of the future.

1. What do you think this writer's task is?

2. What is the central idea?

3. What is one supporting idea in the outline?

4. Find one example of evidence in the outline.

5. If the writer wanted to add another supporting idea to this essay, what could it be?

6. Which supporting idea does this piece of evidence support?
   E-readers offer users the ability to adjust the brightness of a screen to avoid glares.

7. Does this evidence belong in this students outline? Why or why not?
   Studies show that readers have better comprehension when they read a physical book than when they use an e-reader.

EXERCISE 6

Students and parents in your district are complaining that teachers assign too much homework. As the student body president, you have been asked to write a letter urging the district to limit the amount of homework teachers can give.

Set a timer for five minutes and brainstorm what you want to say in your letter. When five minutes are up, circle the ideas you want to use.

Now, use the ideas you brainstormed to create an outline of your letter.

Introduction:

Central idea:

Supporting idea 1:

    Evidence a.

    Evidence b.

Supporting idea 2:

    Evidence a.

    Evidence b.

Conclusion:

EXERCISE 7

Use the outline you created on the previous page to draft your letter to the school board. Write out your ideas in full sentences and add details and transitional phrases.

EXERCISE 8

Before you mail your letter, you want to edit it for spelling, punctuation, and grammar errors. Imagine the paragraph below appeared in your letter. Circle all the mistakes and rewrite it correctly.

Believe it or not, Students are not not the only ones who are impacted by to much homework. Parents are also negatively effected. Parents are also busy. Many parents' work full time jobs, and then when they get Home, they have to help their children do homework. Sometimes parents do not now how to help their children sometimes parents do not have the educationally background to help sometimes parents do not speak the language and sometimes their may only be 1 parent at home to help. Which is stressful. And leds to fighting among the parents and child.

UNIT 3
Chapter
15 RESEARCH FOR WRITING

RESEARCH is the process of gathering information about a specific topic. Strong writing is supported by research.

How do you research for writing? Start with a **RESEARCH QUESTION**. This is the question you will answer using the facts and evidence that you gather in your research. A strong research question is specific and open-ended.

> It doesn't have one simple answer.

Example:

✗ How does social media affect people? ← too broad

✗ How many people use social media? ← too narrow

✗ Is social media bad for you? ← too simple

✓ What effect does social media have on the mental health of teenagers? ← specific, interesting, and complex!

RESEARCH QUESTIONS

An effective research question is:

- **Specific and focused:** It isn't too general or too narrow.
- **Researchable:** It can be answered with data and source material.
- **Relevant:** It applies to a current or timely issue or debate.
- **Complex:** It cannot be answered with a "yes" or "no."
- **Open-ended:** It avoids who, what, when, and where questions.

You answer a research question by gathering evidence from **SOURCES**. Sources can be texts such as books, articles, journal entries, letters, data records, or audio transcripts. They can also be videos, live interviews, multimedia presentations, photographs, art pieces, maps, or speeches. Pretty much anything that can give you reliable, relevant information!

SOURCE
anything that provides information that answers a research question

You can find sources **ONLINE**, in **LIBRARIES**, or in **ARCHIVES**.

If you are doing literary analysis, you still need a research question! The research question will be about the book, and your source is the text you are analyzing.

Example:

✗ Who is Claudia's mother in *The Bluest Eye*?

✗ What is the setting of *The Bluest Eye*?

✓ What do marigolds symbolize in Toni Morrison's novel *The Bluest Eye*?

A source needs to be **CREDIBLE**, which means created by an expert or a reliable author, published by a respected publisher, supported by evidence, and free from **BIAS**.

BIAS
a prejudiced, distorted, or incomplete outlook

Avoid untrustworthy sources such as advertisements, tabloids, personal blogs, social media posts, or sources that don't have a clear author.

Keep a list of all the sources you use and take notes on the information that answers your research question. Be sure to record titles, authors, and page numbers. These notes will become your supporting evidence.

It is important to **CITE** the sources you use. A **CITATION** is a reference to a source that states where the information came from and gives credit to the original authors.

It can be helpful to keep a research notebook dedicated to your notes and sources.

Depending on the kind of source and the citation style, that information can include:

- The title of the work
- The author or creator of the work
- The publisher, or company that distributed it
- The date it was published
- The format of the work (print, video, online)
- Where you can find the quoted material in the work (a page number in a book, or a time stamp for a video)

There are many citation styles, such as MLA, APA, or Chicago. Your teacher will let you know which one to use. Most styles require the same information, but the format of the citation will be different.

Examples:

MLA format

Baptiste, Tracey. *The Jumbies*. Algonquin Young Readers, 2015. Print.

APA format

Baptiste, T. (2015). *The Jumbies*. Algonquin Young Readers.

A **WORKS CITED PAGE** lists citations for all the sources you used in alphabetical order. It comes at the end of a piece of writing.

An **IN-TEXT CITATION** is a shortened citation that appears in the body of a text, immediately after information from that source is used.

Example:

Katherine Johnson was an African American woman who worked for NASA and helped put the first American astronaut into orbit *(Shetterly 6).*   MLA in-text citation

author ↗   ↖ page number

Katherine Johnson was an African American woman who worked for NASA and helped put the first American astronaut into orbit *(Shetterly,* 2016).   APA in-text citation

author ↗   ↖ publication date

All in-text citations refer readers to a full-length citation listed in the works cited page.

THINK:
It is important to check the current rules for citation styles, as the rules are updated often. You can use online tools such as NoodleTools and EasyBib to create accurate works cited pages.

PLAGIARISM is copying original ideas or exact language from a source and using them in your writing as if they were your own. This is against the rules. If you are using another person's original words, you must present them as a quotation and include a citation.

Example:

When people look back on this era of social media and technology, they might say, "It was the best of times, it was the worst of times" (Dickens 1).

quotation

in-text citation

? COMMON KNOWLEDGE

If something is common knowledge, you don't need to cite a source for it. For example, Barack Obama was the first Black president of the United States—everyone knows it! No citation needed. Save citations for original ideas, arguments, data, quotations, or lesser-known facts.

EXERCISE 1

Use your knowledge about writing research questions to explain why each research question below is ineffective.

1. Who invented Google?

2. Is social media bad?

3. How has music evolved over time?

4. What are the effects of climate change?

5. Should people visit Times Square in New York City?

6. What inventions have impacted us today?

EXERCISE 2

Use what you know about writing strong research questions to improve the ones below. Rewrite a strong research question for each topic.

1. Who invented Google?

2. Is social media bad?

3. How has music evolved over time?

4. What are the effects of climate change?

5. Should people visit Times Square in New York City?

6. What inventions have impacted us today?

EXERCISE 3

Your turn! Write your own research questions for the topics provided below.

1. Video games

2. Grades

3. Community service

4. Peer pressure

5. Plastics pollution

EXERCISE 4

Find a credible source for each of the research questions below. Explain why you think the source is trustworthy.

1. How does allowing middle school students to use cell phones in class lead to increased engagement?

2. What are the alternatives to using lab mice to test beauty products?

3. Who were three leading women artists of the Harlem Renaissance?

4. How has social media affected teenagers' perceptions of beauty?

5. What were the roles and responsibilities of women in the Apache Native American tribe in the nineteenth century?

EXERCISE 5

You have a research paper due tomorrow, and you just found a research notebook full of notes about blowing out candles on birthday cakes. Jackpot! Use the research you found to write a short paragraph on the possible risks associated with blowing out candles on a birthday cake. Include a clear central idea, use a minimum of two sources, and cite your information using MLA format.

Title: "Is it Safe to Blow Out Birthday Candles? Here's What Experts Say"
Author: Chrissy Callahan
Publication: 11/3/2020, *TODAY*

"Blowing out candles can expel virus particles, just like breathing, talking, singing, shouting, coughing, and sneezing, if the person is infected."

Quote from Dr. S. Patrick Kachur, professor of population and family health at Columbia University's Mailman School of Public Health

Title: This Is How Disgusting Blowing Out Birthday Candles Is
Author: Bruce Y. Lee
Publication: 8/1/2017, *Forbes*

"Blowing out candles on average resulted in 1,400% (that's 14 times) more bacteria on the frosting. Of course, the amount of bacteria varied depending on the blower."

Title: The Unsettling Truth About Blowing Out Candles on Cake
Author: Mayukh Sen
Publication: 7/28/2017, *Food52*

- Clemson University study simulated blowing out birthday candles and measured bacteria that was left over
- 11 research subjects asked to "blow out candles until they doused the tiny flames"
- 17 candles evenly spaced on a Styrofoam cake
- experiment replicated 3 times on separate days
- Findings: blowing out candles = 15x more bacteria left on the cake, on average compared to control samples

EXERCISE 6

Review the citations below. Label each part of the citation using the words in the word bank. Then, state what kind of source you think it is citing.

Psst! You will not use every term for each citation.

> author   title   publisher   location   publication date   link
> date accessed   type of source   page number   publication

1. Thomas, Angie. 2017. *The Hate U Give.* London: Walker Books.
   _____

2. Jones, Leo A. "Brain Games." *The Scientific Youth* (online). May 13, 2021. Accessed June 15, 2022.
   _____

3. Schmidt, Sarah. "Companies Fail the Test; Junk Food Marketing Aimed at Kids Faulted." *The Gazette* [Montreal], March 10, 2010, p. A.11.

4. Chen, James. "Industrial Revolution Definition: History, Pros, and Cons." *Investopedia*, October 2, 2022, www.investopedia.com/terms/i/industrial-revolution.asp.

5. Beyoncé. "Beyoncé—Pretty Hurts (Video)." Video posted on YouTube, April 24, 2014, www.youtube.com/watch?v=LXXQLa-5n5w.

EXERCISE 7

Use what you know about research to answer the questions below.

1. What is the first step of writing a research paper?

2. What makes an effective research question?

3. Why is it important to use credible sources in a research paper?

4. How can you determine if a source is credible?

5. Why is it important to give credit to your sources? How can you show your audience that you gave credit to your sources?

6. What is plagiarism? How do you avoid it?

Chapter 16 MEDIA LITERACY

MEDIA is a way of communicating information and ideas to lots of people. It includes things like social media posts, websites, street art, video games, television shows, newspapers, ads, commercials, music streaming platforms, and more.

MEDIA LITERACY is the ability to understand and think critically about the media we see and hear every day. It helps us make sense of the information we come across and decide what to believe.

Being media-literate consumers means paying attention to how words, pictures, and sounds are put together to grab our attention and make us think and feel a certain way.

To be media literate, follow these five steps:

1. Understand: When you engage with a piece of media, try to grasp the main points and think about why they're important. Ask yourself questions like: Who made this? What am I learning? How does it make me feel? Who might find it helpful?

2. Analyze: Think about why it was created and what it is saying. Ask questions like: What are they trying to convince me of? Who might disagree with it? What are they not telling me?

3. Question: Don't assume the media you engage with is credible. Instead, prove to yourself that it is. Fact-check information from different sources. Ask: Is it stating facts or opinions? Is there evidence to support this point of view?

4. Recognize bias: Think about the creator's perspective. Notice if they share only one side of the story. Ask: Why did they create this? What information is missing? Do I agree or disagree with their perspective? How does it affect what I think?

Media: Truth and Lies

Sometimes individuals or groups (like companies, or governments) use media to manipulate people. They use it to spread false information by changing images and videos or creating persuasive false stories that benefit their interests. It's important to be aware of these techniques and look for the facts instead of believing everything we see, hear, or read.

When we exercise our media literacy skills, we can avoid being tricked by:

MISINFORMATION	DISINFORMATION	SELECTIVE EDITING
IMAGE MANIPULATION	ASTROTURFING	CLICKBAIT AND SENSATIONALISM

By being media literate, we can make informed choices, protect ourselves from being tricked, and become responsible users of media. It's all about thinking critically, asking questions, and being smart about the media we consume and create.

EXERCISE 1

Sort the words in the word bank into two categories:
MEDIA or **NOT MEDIA.**

newspapers   candy wrappers   road signs
Public Broadcasting Service (PBS)   magazines   TikTok
Spotify   street graffiti   podcasts   anime   butterflies
Mother Nature   Netflix   email   furniture   graphic novels
clothes   YouTube   commercials   cave drawings
birthday card   snow   UNO (card game)   slogan

MEDIA	NOT MEDIA

EXERCISE 2

Review this post and answer the questions to gain a better understanding of it.

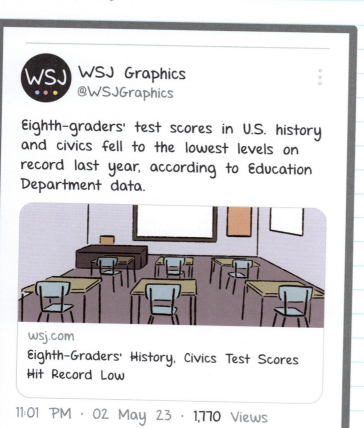

WSJ Graphics
@WSJGraphics

Eighth-graders' test scores in U.S. history and civics fell to the lowest levels on record last year, according to Education Department data.

wsj.com
Eighth-Graders' History, Civics Test Scores Hit Record Low

11:01 PM · 02 May 23 · 1,770 Views

1. Who created the post?

2. What does it consist of?

3. What technique is used to attract your attention?

4. What did you learn from this post?

5. What information is missing that would be important to know?

6. Who might find this post helpful and valuable?

7. Whose perspective is left out?

EXERCISE 3

Analyze this piece of media by answering the questions.

1. Describe the media.
   • What type of media is this?
   • What does it show?

2. Identify the source.

   a. Can you tell where the media comes from?

   b. Who do you think paid to have it created?

3. Interpret the message.

   a. What is the media trying to get you to think or do?

   b. Who was it made for?

   c. What information is missing?

EXERCISE 4

Read each question carefully and choose the best answer.

1. What is bias in media?

   A. A type of superhero
   B. A one-sided view or preference in media
   C. When media shows both sides of a story

2. Which of the following is an example of biased language?

   A. "Everyone should exercise regularly for good health."
   B. "Some people believe exercising is beneficial, while others don't."
   C. "Exercising is a waste of time and doesn't make a difference."

3. Look at the headline below. Is it an example of biased or unbiased language?

   "Amazing New Invention Set to Revolutionize the World!"

   A. Biased
   B. Unbiased

4. Imagine a news article that presents only one side of an argument, without considering opposing viewpoints. Is this an example of biased or unbiased reporting?

   A. Biased
   B. Unbiased

5. How can cultural sensitivity be demonstrated in media?

    A. By including diverse perspectives and representing different cultures accurately

    B. By using exaggerated stereotypes to make people laugh

    C. By promoting one culture over others

6. You see a photograph in a magazine that portrays a particular group of people in a negative way, perpetuating stereotypes. What should you do?

    A. Ignore it and continue reading

    B. Share it with your friends to discuss the stereotypes

    C. Recognize it as biased and consider the harm it may cause

7. True or false: Being aware of bias in media helps us become better critical thinkers and decision-makers.

    A. True

    B. False

Answer yes or no to the questions about this article. Use your yes and no responses to help respond to the final question about the credibility of the source.

Alien Sighting Confirmed in Central Park

Published Yesterday | Alerts

NEW YORK—Late last night, exciting reports describing unusual activity in Manhattan's skyline came pouring in. According to witnesses, somewhere between 10:48 p.m. and 12:25 a.m. either a glowing orb or a massive silver saucer descended from the sky, probably landing somewhere in Central Park. "It was definitely an alien ship," reports one such sharp-eyed New Yorker, who says he was out walking his dog when he saw the spacecraft in the sky. "I saw a little green creature walking down 5th Avenue with my own two eyes!" says another source, who confirmed she was out stargazing in the park when the event happened. This is the latest in a string of confirmed extraterrestrial events that have happened in urban, suburban, and rural areas all over the country. It's only a matter of time until the world must accept—not only are aliens real, but they're here!

	YES	NO	QUESTIONS
1.			Is the author identified?
2.			Are claims supported by evidence (facts)?
3.			Does the media leave out information that would help you better understand the issue?
4.			Is the purpose of the media clear?
5.			Would you be comfortable citing this source in a research assignment?
6.			Does the media contain false or misleading information?
7.			Can you confirm any of the information from personal knowledge or another source?

Based on the yes and no responses, write one reason to trust or distrust this media.

Read this student blog post and answer the questions.

Posted today • 15 Comments

Standardized Tests Don't Meet My Standards!!

As an 8th grader, I've been in middle school for a few years now. Each year ends with a stressful week when students are bombarded with test, after test, after test! Math, English, Science, and Social Studies. These are standardized tests.

What is a standardized test you ask? It's any test that is given to students in a standard way—same length, same questions, same rubric. Which pretty much covers all tests, even pop quizzes. However, when students hear "standardized test" they think of the big tests at the end of the year, given to kids all across a state. They also think: STRESS!

For one thing, they test us on SO much material, it's really hard to fit it all in one school year. If you want to take your time to understand something, forget it! You have to keep moving. We spend at least a month studying and taking practice tests, but you never know what the test will focus on, so you have to prepare for EVERYTHING. If you study something hard, there's no guarantee it'll be covered. Example: I spent a lot of time studying the Mongol Empire (which was a super influential empire, by the way!) but my World History test didn't even ask about them once.

Now, multiply all that preparation and stress by four subjects. Yeah. And remember, all these tests happen in the same week. Everyone tells us to get lots of sleep so we are sharp and ready, but how can we sleep when we need to study one year's worth of material for at least four classes, all at the same time? This year I was so tired, I fell asleep during my last test! Thankfully, I still did okay. Oh, and it was 95 degrees that day. Do you think my testing room had air conditioning? Nope.

Is this "standard" measurement of student success an accurate one? I don't think so. . . .

1. What did you learn about the author?

2. Why do you think the author wrote this?

3. What is missing from the message?

4. How might different people interpret this message?

5. Who might benefit from this message?

EXERCISE 7

Are these actions helpful when analyzing media and its messages? Answer yes or no.

1. _____ Learning who created the media and how they sourced their information

2. _____ Checking the language used and what emotions it is trying to evoke

3. _____ Identifying the lessons the author of the media learned from others

4. _____ Fact-checking against other credible sources

5. _____ Ignoring stereotyping since most media contains it

6. _____ Checking your feelings about what you saw, heard, or read

7. _____ Understanding why the media was created

8. _____ Knowing whether the media's author was born before or after you

9. _____ Seeing any prior drafts or revisions of the media

10. _____ Understanding how the media was made

EXERCISE 8

Read each question carefully and select the most appropriate answer.

1. What is media manipulation?

   A. Using media to communicate information effectively
   B. Altering images and videos for artistic purposes
   C. Influencing or controlling media to deceive or manipulate people

2. Which of the following is an example of media manipulation?

   A. Creating engaging advertisements
   B. Using colorful graphics in a news article
   C. Spreading false information to sway public opinion

3. What is clickbait?

   A. A type of advertising banner
   B. Catchy headlines used to attract readers' attention
   C. Online games and quizzes

4. Which tactic is commonly used to manipulate emotions in media?

   A. Presenting factual information
   B. Using logical arguments
   C. Employing sensationalism and exaggeration

5. What is the purpose of media manipulation?

    A. To entertain the audience
    B. To control or influence people's beliefs and actions
    C. To educate and inform the public

6. Which term refers to creating false social media accounts to promote a certain agenda?

    A. Trolling
    B. Meme creation
    C. Astroturfing

7. How can you identify media manipulation?

    A. By analyzing sources and cross-checking information
    B. By believing everything you see or hear
    C. By ignoring any conflicting viewpoints

8. What can you do to protect yourself from media manipulation?

    A. Share sensational news stories on social media
    B. Rely solely on a single news source
    C. Verify information and think critically before accepting something as true

9. Why is it important to understand media manipulation?

    A. To become a discerning consumer and creator of information
    B. To create engaging content on social media
    C. To control and manipulate others' opinions

BONUS QUESTION! Think about your day today. What kinds of media have you interacted with? List as many as you can think of!

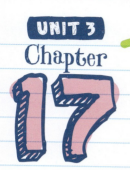

EXPOSITORY WRITING

EXPOSITORY WRITING is nonfiction writing that informs, describes, defines, or explains facts to a specific audience. There are two main types to know:

INFORMATIVE writing conveys information or your knowledge about a topic.

Format Examples:
encyclopedias, newspaper articles, magazine articles, textbooks, brochures, pamphlets, interviews

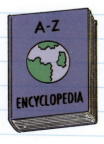

Topic Examples:
What is the history of fast food in the United States?

What is ChatGPT?

How did social influencers get their start?

EXPLANATORY writing offers explanations, provides answers, and evaluates information.

Format Examples:
self-help books, blogs, cookbooks, recipes, guides, manuals, directions

Topic Examples:
How has fast food impacted the health of American society?

How will ChatGPT affect education?

How do social influencers affect teen behavior?

Let's say you have been tasked to write an essay informing middle schoolers about a strategy they can use to take care of their mental health.

Writers can use both informative writing and explanatory writing in the same essay to complete their task.

Here's how you might structure your essay.

1. Introduce the Topic

Grab your audience's attention with an interesting **HOOK**, a quick glimpse of what they will encounter in your writing.

Hook Example:

Have you ever had thoughts about yourself like "you're bad at everything" or "don't try, you'll just fail"? It's not a kind way to talk about yourself. Imagine if someone said those things to your little sister or your best friend.

Then, state your **CENTRAL IDEA**.

Example:

A healthy mindset is essential for mental health. We can create habits that help us adjust and control our mindset.

2. Develop the Topic

Develop your central idea with supporting ideas and **EVIDENCE**—facts and information, such as definitions, details, quotations, or examples.

Expository writing often uses **DOMAIN-SPECIFIC VOCABULARY**—words that are specific to a particular subject or field. And remember, it is always helpful to define or explain any terms your audience may not know.

Example:

Some domain-specific vocabulary to include in your essay might be "fixed mindset" and "growth mindset."

Use these **MODES OF DEVELOPMENT** to expand on your central idea.

MODE OF DEVELOPMENT	FUNCTION	EXAMPLE
Definition	Explaining an unfamiliar word, term, or concept	**Mindset:** a set of beliefs that shape how you make sense of the world and yourself
Classification	Organizing items into categories to show relationships	There are three kinds of mindsets: fixed mindset, growth mindset, and benefit mindset.
Comparison	Examining the similarities and differences between two or more items	Having a **growth mindset** means that you believe your intelligence and talents can be developed over time. Having a **fixed mindset** means that you believe intelligence and talents are predetermined and cannot be changed.
Cause and effect	Noting the relationship between two things when one makes the other thing happen	A growth mindset causes new neural pathways to grow in the brain.

MODE OF DEVELOPMENT	FUNCTION	EXAMPLE
Narration	Telling a story or anecdote to illustrate a point	Leo was coming in last in every race, until he decided to change his mindset. Instead of winning, he focused on enjoying practice. Three weeks later, he came in second.
Process analysis	Informing your audience how to do something or how something works	First the brain experiences a chemical change. Next, neurons light up new paths that change the brain's structure. Finally, with repeated exposure, those neural pathways strengthen and become permanent.
Description	Using the five senses to help readers understand the topic	Carol S. Dwerk writes: "Confronted with hard puzzles, one ten-year-old boy pulled up his chair, rubbed his hands together, smacked his lips, and cried, 'I love a challenge!'"

MODE OF DEVELOPMENT	FUNCTION	EXAMPLE
Example	Explaining your subject with examples that show your audience its nature or character	Jimmy is struggling with sixth-grade math. He has a fixed mindset and believes he will never be good at math.

3. Finish with a Conclusion

Summarize the ideas and evidence you presented and end on a powerful note. How can the reader learn more? How can they get involved or make a change? How can they think or act differently?

Example:

In the long run, a growth mindset can lead to success in all areas of life. So, the next time you're struggling with something, remember: Failure is part of getting better. Shift your mindset!

EXERCISE 1

Read each passage and decide whether it is an example of informative writing, explanatory writing, or a combination of both. Explain your answer.

1. To make an omelet, crack two to three eggs in a mixing bowl (depending on how hungry you are). Next, beat the eggs with a fork until the whites and the yolks are blended and the mixture is smooth. Test it by scooping up some of the mixture on a fork. If it's gloppy, keep beating! When it's smooth, add a big pinch of salt. Heat an 8-inch pan on medium heat and melt a pad of butter in it. When the butter is melted, pour your egg mixture into the pan.

2. Pocket mice are the tiniest mice in North America, weighing between six and ten grams. (That's about the weight of three pennies!) They could fit in your pocket, but they are named for the fur-lined pouches on the outside of their cheeks, which they use to carry food and building materials for their tiny nests. These little mice are endangered—scientists even thought they were extinct for a while. They used to live along the Pacific Coast, from California to Mexico, but as humans built houses and businesses by the beach, their habitats began to disappear.

3. Here are two life-changing acne prevention tips. One: Change your pillowcase at least once a week. Pillowcases are teeming with bacteria and oils from our hair and skin. Every time you put your face on one, pimple-causing bacteria is rubbed right into your pores! Two: Don't dry your face with a used towel. As soon as a wet towel begins to dry, bacteria start to grow. If you use that towel later, you're just rubbing bacteria onto your freshly washed face! Use a clean towel or a fresh paper towel, every time.

4. Next time you're feeling anxious, follow these steps to help keep you grounded. Look around your environment. Name five things you see. Then, name four things you can touch. Next, name three things you can hear. Then, name two things you can smell. Finally, name one thing you can taste.

5. Making TikTok content for brands is the hot new gig. Billions of people use the app every month. As the social media platform's popularity continues to grow, brands are hiring college students and other young people—sometimes with pay and sometimes with college credits—to help them create content that will go viral.

EXERCISE 2

Read each example and identify which mode of development is being used.

definition   description   classification   cause and effect
narration   comparison   process analysis   example

1. To combat bullying in school, it is important for teachers and administrators to recognize the three types of bullying: physical, verbal, and social.

_____

2. Vaping can be harmful to the body by, for instance, damaging small passageways in the lungs.

_____

3. One of the differences between middle school and high school is the level of freedom and independence students experience.

_____

4. Signs of substance abuse may include uneven skin tone, chapped lips, and dark spots.

_____

5. On TikTok, viewers can watch three kinds of videos: _____
   social media challenges, tutorials, and influencer
   collaborations.

6. Mindfulness is the act of slowing down and focusing _____
   on the moment.

7. Procrastination can be caused by perfectionism, _____
   fear of failure, or fear of criticism.

8. I remember the first time I had to deliver a speech _____
   to an audience. It was in kindergarten during a
   "show and tell."

9. *The Giver*, *The Hunger Games*, and *The Maze Runner* _____
   all fall into the dystopian genre.

10. There are three steps to becoming a more _____
    confident speaker.

**Read the excerpts from *World Without Fish* by
Mark Kurlansky. Respond to the questions below.**

Most of the fish we commonly eat, most of the fish we know, could be
gone in the next fifty years. This includes salmon, tuna, cod, swordfish, and
anchovies. If this happens, many other fish that depend on these fish will
also be in trouble. So will seabirds that eat fish, such as seagulls and cormo-
rants. So will mammals that eat fish, such as whales, porpoises, and seals.
And insects that depend on seabirds, such as beetles and lizards. Slowly—or
maybe not so slowly—in less time than the several billion years it took to
create it—life on planet Earth could completely unravel.

1. What is the central idea in this excerpt?

2. How does Kurlansky use cause and effect in this passage to achieve
his purpose?

3. What is one example Kurlansky provides? How does the example illustrate
his point?

People who are in school today are lucky to have been born at a special moment in history. The Industrial Revolution, beginning in the mid-eighteenth century and continuing for the next 120 years, shifted production from handcrafts to machine-made factory goods and in so doing completely changed the relationship of people to nature, the relationship of people to each other, politics, art, and architecture—the look and thought of the world. In the next fifty years, much of your working life, there will be as much change in less than half the time. The future of the world, perhaps even the survival of the planet, will depend on how well these changes are handled. And so you have more opportunities and more responsibilities than any other generation in history.

4. Who is Kurlansky's intended audience? How do you know?

5. What mode of development does Kurlansky use in this excerpt? How does it help him achieve his purpose?

One of the great thinkers of the Industrial Revolution was an Englishman named Charles Darwin. In 1859, he had published one of the most important books ever written: *On the Origin of Species by Means of Natural Selection, or the Preservation of Favoured Races in the Struggle for Life*, more commonly known by its shortened title: *On the Origin of Species*.

In his book, Darwin explained the order of nature as a system in which all the many various plants and animal species struggle for survival. He did not see nature as particularly nice or kind, but as a cruel system in which species attempted to kill and dominate other species in order to secure the survival of their own kind. He wrote, "We do not see, or we forget, that the birds which are idly singing round us, mostly live on insects or seeds, and are thus constantly destroying life."

6. Why does Kurlansky include the reference to Darwin? How does this source of information support his central idea?

Plants and animals are organized into groups with seven major levels or categories: kingdom, phylum, class, order, family, genus (plural: genera), species.

7. What mode of development is used in this excerpt?

A codfish and a human belong to the same kingdom, which is animals. They also belong to the same phylum, which is vertebrates (animals with spines). But after that, they break off into completely different classes—cod are fish and humans are mammals. More specifically, humans are vertebrates of the class known as mammals in the order known as primates, which we share with monkeys and lemurs. We belong to the family Hominidae, which we share with apes and chimpanzees. Within that family, we are of the genus *Homo*, which are Hominidae that walk standing up on two feet. . . . Cod, on the other hand, are fish—specifically fish with jaws—that belong to a family called Gadidae. This fish family is fairly evolved, has elaborate fins, and lives in the bottom part of the ocean. They hunt voraciously the species living directly over and beneath them, and have white flesh greatly favored by *Homo sapiens.*

8. What mode of development is used in this excerpt?

9. Is the above excerpt an example of informative or explanatory writing?

EXERCISE 4

Read the excerpt from a student's essay. Write a brief response in which you identify the central idea and discuss how two modes of development help the author achieve their purpose.

It was 10 p.m. on a Sunday night, and I had a five-page research paper to write. I had three weeks to draft it, but there I was staring at a blank screen. I had procrastinated, and now I was doomed. I thought, wouldn't it be amazing if there were a machine that could write my paper for me? I'm sure that many students like me have had a similar sentiment at one point during their academic careers. However, for students in the future, this dream will soon be a reality. With the new AI technology, known as ChatGPT, writing will not be such a daunting task. This revolutionary technology will change the way people communicate.

ChatGPT is artificial intelligence that can give sophisticated human responses to user inputs. This versatile tool can do many tasks: pen an email, compose a joke, explain complex problems, write a term paper, generate business strategies, compose a song, or help plan a vacation. It can even provide recommendations such as movie suggestions based on your preferences! Although there have been chatbots before, their responses were often inconsistent and inaccurate at times. ChatGPT, on the other hand, is much more impressive. The intelligence is so advanced that even top film and television writers are worried that their jobs will be jeopardized.

BONUS QUESTION! Do you think ChatGPT is a useful tool? Why or why not? On a separate piece of paper use two modes of development to explain your answer.

EXERCISE 5

Think of an invention that has changed lives. Write a few sentences about this topic through each mode of development.

MODE OF DEVELOPMENT	EXAMPLE
Definition	
Classification	
Comparison and contrast	
Cause and effect	

MODE OF DEVELOPMENT	EXAMPLE
Narration	
Process analysis	
Description	
Example	

Write an informative or explanatory paragraph about the invention you explored in exercise 5. Come up with a central idea, use at least two modes of development, and cite any sources you use.

Here are some ideas:

- Write about the way the invention has changed or improved life.
- Write about how the invention works.
- Write about the positive or negative aspects of the invention.
- Write about the way to use or operate the invention.
- Write about the way the invention has improved over time.
- Write about why the invention may be better than a previous one.
- Write about ways to use the invention safely.

EXERCISE 7

Match the subject, topic, or activity with the correct set of domain-specific vocabulary words.

Psst! If you're stuck, look up one of the domain-specific vocabulary words in a dictionary!

1. Chemistry _____

2. Rapping _____

3. Fishing _____

4. Cooking _____

5. Medicine _____

6. Aviation _____

7. Astronomy _____

8. Bowling _____

9. Swimming _____

10. Math _____

A. Backstroke, freestyle, float

B. Sauté, broil, sear

C. Zenith, constellation, eclipse

D. Division, quotient, sum

E. Angler, downrigger, bait

F. Rudder, runway, descent

G. Freestyle, bars, flow

H. Abrasion, abscess, blood clot

I. Atom, catalyst, electron

J. Strike, spare, pins

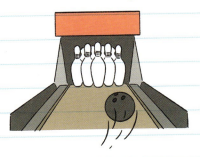

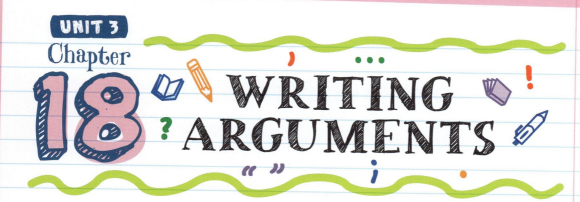

UNIT 3
Chapter 18
WRITING ARGUMENTS

PERSUASIVE writing and **ARGUMENTATIVE** writing both make claims about a topic.

PERSUASIVE writing supports a claim using appeals to emotion. The goal is to <u>convince</u> the reader that your position is the right one, not to <u>prove</u> it.

> **TYPES OF PERSUASIVE WRITING:**
> advertisements, commercials, editorials, persuasive essays, campaign and persuasive speeches, and book or movie reviews

Example:

Efforts to end summer reading programs should not be supported! My library's summer reading program was one of my favorite parts of last year's summer vacation. I read so many wonderful books I never would have read otherwise, and I bonded with my new best friend. Would you really want to rob children of these life-changing experiences?

> The writer's tone is informal. They focus on thoughts and feelings.

ARGUMENTATIVE writing proves a claim with reason and evidence. The goal is to get your reader to see your point as valid whether they agree with it or not.

Example:

Summer reading is a longstanding tradition that encourages good reading habits and prevents summer learning loss. However, many parents and students are pushing back against summer reading assignments. While these critics contend that students need a break from schoolwork, there are many valuable benefits of summer reading programs, and they should continue to be practiced in school districts.

The writer's tone is neutral. They focus on facts and logical points.

In ancient Greece, a philosopher named Aristotle observed that there are three **ARGUMENTATIVE APPEALS**. We still use these appeals to make strong, convincing arguments.

HMM . . . SEEMS LIKE I MADE A PRETTY STRONG ARGUMENT!

APPEALS
specific strategies used to present claims, facts, examples, and arguments

think "**log**ic"

Aristotle

A **LOGOS** appeal relies on reason, clear thinking, and facts to support a claim.

think "**eth**ics"

An **ETHOS** appeal establishes the writer's character as trustworthy.

think "em**pathy**"

A **PATHOS** appeal relies on the emotions, beliefs, and values of the audience.

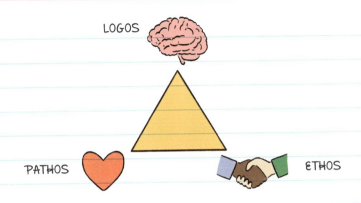

LOGOS

PATHOS

ETHOS

Example:

ethos

As an experienced veterinarian, I recommend adopting your next pet from an animal shelter, rather than purchasing it from a store. Hundreds of thousands of adorable furry friends are euthanized each year because not enough people have it in their hearts to adopt. And for no good reason! One of the biggest benefits of _pathos_ adopting is the cost. You can save hundreds of dollars, and do a good thing for animals in need at the same time. _logos_

Argumentative writing is formal and follows a strict structure. It's important to follow this structure so your argument makes sense.

INTRODUCTION:

An opening statement or passage that provides any background information to position your argument

CLAIM:

The point you are making in your argumentative writing

In persuasive writing, your reasons may be supported by anecdotes, or appeals to emotions and morality.

REASONS:
Specific points that support, explain, and/or prove your claim

Your evidence should be cited from credible sources.

EVIDENCE:
Facts, statistics, or expert testimonies that support your argument

COUNTERCLAIM:
A viewpoint that opposes your claim

REBUTTAL:
Evidence and reasons that show the opposing viewpoint is incorrect

CONCLUSION:
A closing passage that restates your claim and summarizes your argument

In persuasive writing, the conclusion may be a call to action or a statement of what you hope the audience will do, think, or believe after reading.

PERSUASIVE WRITING
Persuasive writing might include some of these components, but it doesn't have to include all of them, and the organization might be different.

Counterclaim Strategies

Addressing an opposing viewpoint shows your readers that you are well-educated on a topic, which makes your argument more valid.

also called a "counterargument"

A **COUNTERCLAIM** is a position that goes against, or opposes, your main argument.

A **CONCESSION** is acknowledging that a counterclaim is true or valid to an extent.

also called a "refutation"

A **REBUTTAL** is a response to a counterclaim that shows why the counterargument is wrong or flawed.

Example:

claim

Elementary school students should not have to do homework. Many argue that homework is necessary for students to *counterclaim* learn essential skills. And though it may give students extra time to practice, there is no research that proves homework *concession* has academic benefits to children before high school. *rebuttal*

THINK:
When you introduce a COUNTERCLAIM or make a CONCESSION, you <u>must</u> follow up with a REBUTTAL that supports your claim. Otherwise bringing it up won't help prove your point!

Read the situations below. State whether each task requires **ARGUMENTATIVE** writing or **PERSUASIVE** writing.

1. Write an editorial for the school newspaper motivating students to donate used coats for charity this winter.
   _____

2. Who is responsible for the tragedy in the play, Macbeth or the witches? Write an essay that supports your position.
   _____

3. Was the United States justified in dropping bombs on Hiroshima and Nagasaki during the Second World War? Write an essay that supports your position.
   _____

4. You loved *Wednesday*, Netflix's hilarious supernatural-mystery show. Write a review encouraging your classmates to watch it.
   _____

5. A company wants to tear down a historical site in your town and replace it with a fast-food restaurant. Write an article that shows why the local government should stop them.
   _____

6. The food bank you volunteer at needs more help. ----------------------
Your principal is letting you make an announcement over the intercom, inviting students to volunteer.

7. You are writing a letter to the school board ----------------------
arguing that students should have more opportunities for extra credit.

8. You purchased a T-shirt online, and there was ----------------------
a hole in it! Write to the company asking for a refund.

EXERCISE 2

These sentences are from a student's argumentative essay about the necessity for snow days. Identify which part of an argument each sentence is.

> introduction   claim   reason   evidence
> counterclaim   concession   rebuttal   conclusion

1. Teenagers are experiencing high levels of stress, _____ and snow days provide necessary breaks that students need.

2. The critics of snow days believe that technology _____ can help recover the lost instruction time that snow days take away.

3. The forecasters are predicting a winter storm, _____ the first of the season, and students, parents, and teachers are checking the forecast throughout the evening wondering just one thing: Will there be a snow day?

4. Access to internet and technology is not universal, _____ and some students might fall behind if they aren't able to adapt to remote learning unexpectedly.

Psst! You will use some parts of an argument more than once.

5. In her article, Patricia Smith cites a 2018 ----------------------
Pew Research poll in which "70 percent of
teenagers said anxiety and depression were
major problems among their peers."

6. It may be true that technology can facilitate ----------------------
remote instruction time.

7. Despite access to technology that makes remote ----------------------
learning an option when the weather is bad,
snow days are still a valuable tradition, and
important to keep.

8. To summarize, just because the technology exists ----------------------
to teach students remotely does not mean it
should be used to take away snow days.

9. A recent EdWeek Research Center survey found ----------------------
that more than 2 million students in the United
States are not equipped to learn from home.

10. However, it does not guarantee that remote ----------------------
instruction will be effective, especially when the
switch to remote learning is unexpected, or
last minute.

Read the persuasive letter below and respond to the questions that follow.

Dear Mom and Mama,

Over the past few summers, you have been so kind to take us on awesome family vacations. I'm the luckiest kid alive!

I know you are talking about taking a cruise this year, but I'm hoping you will consider a cross-country road trip instead. I think it would be so cool to travel to a bunch of states we've never been to and see historical sites I've learned about in history class. Also, I've heard road trips are cheaper than cruises, just saying.

Best of all, we'd get to spend even more time together! If we go on a cruise, I'll probably make friends my own age and end up hanging out with them more than you. I'd rather spend my time riding in the car, singing along to the radio, and talking about life as a family. I won't be young forever. Soon I'll be off to college and out of the house. Wouldn't it be fun to make this special memory together before I get too old?

Think about it!

Love,
Me

1. Who is the writer's audience?

2. What is the writer's claim?

3. Name one reason the writer gives to support their claim.

4. What argumentative appeals does this writer use? Give an example.

5. Does the writer include a counterclaim?

6. Pretend you are the writer's audience. Did this letter persuade you? Why or why not?

Read the argumentative essay below and respond to the questions that follow.

Many parents and students across the country are pushing back against assigned summer reading. While critics contend that summer vacation should be a time of rest for students, there are many valuable benefits to continue reading during the summer including the prevention of summer learning loss and enhancing student achievement.

Summer reading can prevent "summer slide." As students return to school this fall after an eight-week vacation, many of them will be starting the academic year with achievement levels lower than where they were at the beginning of summer break. This phenomenon—sometimes referred to as summer learning loss, summer setback, or summer slide—has been of interest to education researchers going back as far as 1906 (Cooper). David M. Quinn, Assistant Professor of Education at the University of Southern California, summarized several findings regarding summer slide and noted ways to combat the problem. In the report "Summer Learning Loss: What Is It and What Can Be Done About It?" he found that "on average, students' achievement scores declined over summer vacation by one month's worth of school-year learning."

Despite all the benefits reading may bring, many parents and students do not see summer reading as pleasure but rather as another task to be completed. This complaint is true to some extent. For most students, their summer reading experience has been mostly comprised of stale reading title suggestions created by teachers in a last-ditch effort to make reading fun and exciting.

However, current research and best practices have indicated that the only way students will truly embrace reading over the summer is if they are presented with *choice*. Similar studies show that when students are given the opportunity to choose their own reading titles, they will become more engaged.

1. What is the writer's argument?

2. What reasons does the writer provide to support the claim?

3. What type of supporting evidence does the writer use in this essay?

4. What counterclaim does the writer address?

5. What is the writer's rebuttal? Do they use a concession?

KEEP READING!

EXERCISE 5

Read the passages below. State which argumentative appeal each passage uses: logos, ethos, or pathos. Underline the **WORDS** and **PHRASES** that help you decide.

Psst! Some passages might use more than one!

1. If you are having a hard time getting enough exercise each day, you might want to consider getting a dog. According to the American Heart Association, dog owners are 54 percent more likely to get the recommended amount of exercise than people who don't own dogs.

2. Social media can distort our perception of reality, which for many people can trigger depressive moods and make anxiety worse. As a licensed therapist, I advise my patients who are experiencing anxiety or depression to consider reducing or eliminating social media usage.

3. Middle schools and high schools should have later start times. Pediatricians say that teens need at least nine hours of sleep a night for their brains to function. With many extracurricular activities letting out as late as 7:00 p.m., and hours of homework to complete each night, it's not possible for students to keep up with their responsibilities and get enough sleep. Especially if they have to wake up as early as 5:30 a.m. to get to school on time.

4. Being bullied day in and day out is torture. It is scary and isolating and humiliating. Many students don't know where to turn and might be worried that asking for help will make things worse. We must find a way to get these students the help they need. Looking the other way will only make things worse for everyone.

5. After six years of playing soccer, believe me, one of the most important things you can do to improve your skills is to stretch. Stretch before every practice and every game. Stretch when you wake up and before you go to sleep. You will not only increase your range of motion, but you will be less likely to get injured.

6. Please let me go to the concert! I know it's on a school night, but it's my favorite band! They've never done a show this close to home before, and I might never have an opportunity like this again. It would mean the world to me if you let me go. Don't you remember what it was like to be a teenager and want to go to your first concert?

In 2019, teen environmental activist Greta Thunberg spoke to world leaders at the United Nations about climate change. Read an excerpt from that speech below and respond to the questions that follow.

You have stolen my dreams and my childhood with your empty words and yet I'm one of the lucky ones. People are suffering. People are dying. Entire ecosystems are collapsing. We are in the beginning of a mass extinction, and all you can talk about is money and fairy tales of eternal economic growth. How dare you!

For more than 30 years, the science has been crystal clear. How dare you continue to look away and come here saying that you're doing enough when the politics and solutions needed are still nowhere in sight.

You say you hear us and that you understand the urgency. But no matter how sad and angry I am, I do not want to believe that. Because if you really understood the situation and still kept on failing to act, then you would be evil. And that I refuse to believe.

The popular idea of cutting our emissions in half in 10 years only gives us a 50 percent chance of staying below 1.5 degrees [Celsius] and the risk of setting off irreversible chain reactions beyond human control.

Fifty percent may be acceptable to you, but those numbers do not include tipping points, most feedback loops, additional warming hidden by toxic air pollution or the aspects of equity and climate justice. They also rely on my generation sucking hundreds of billions of tons of your CO_2 out of the air with technologies that barely exist.

So a 50 percent risk is simply not acceptable to us—we who have to live with the consequences. . . .

1. What is Greta Thunberg's claim?

2. How does Thunberg appeal to ethos? Provide one example and explain how it is effective.

3. How does Thunberg appeal to logos? Provide one example and explain how it is effective.

4. How does Thunberg appeal to pathos? Provide one example and explain how it is effective.

5. Is Thunberg's speech an example of argumentative writing or persuasive writing? Why?

EXERCISE 7

It's the end of the quarter. You currently have an average of 89 percent in your English class. Write an email to your teacher persuading them to bump your grade up one percentage point to an A. Use ethos, logos, and pathos to make your argument persuasive.

EXERCISE 8

Your turn! Use the writing process to brainstorm, outline, and draft an argumentative essay.

First, brainstorm your topic. What causes or issues are you passionate about? What do you wish more people believed? Brainstorm argument ideas below.

Use the ideas you brainstormed to come up with the central idea you will structure your essay around.

Central idea:

Brainstorm take two! What supporting arguments could you use to prove your point? Jot them down below.

EXERCISE 9

Make a plan! Organize your strongest ideas into an outline using the template below.

I.

   a.

   b.

II.

   a.

   b.

III.

   a.

   b.

IV.

   a.

   b.

EXERCISE 10

Now turn that outline into a first draft! Use full sentences and add transitions to help keep your ideas organized.

UNIT 1
Grammar

Exercise 1

1. E
2. D
3. B
4. G
5. C
6. H
7. A
8. F

Exercise 2

1. Preposition
2. Verb
3. Adjective
4. Adverb
5. Adverb
6. Noun
7. Verb
8. Preposition
9. Verb
10. Noun

Exercise 3

1. Phrase
2. Clause
3. Phrase
4. Phrase
5. Clause
6. Phrase
7. Clause
8. Clause
9. Phrase
10. Clause

Exercise 4

phrase | clause

1 After the storm, the campers continued their hike.

2 The teacher lectured the pranksters about their unruly behavior.

3 The students played foursquare on the blacktop.

4 In the forest, there was little light.

5 The dirt bike skidded across the gravel.

6 Throughout the performance, the child fidgeted.

7 The chocolate ice cream dripped on her white vest.

8 There is a huge sale on LeBron sneakers!

9 The fruit bat slept peacefully until sunset.

10 Tricia found her Earth Science classroom on the second floor.

BONUS QUESTION: 10 (All of them are independent clauses!)

Exercise 5

1 Dependent clause

2 Dependent clause

3 Independent clause

4 Dependent clause

5 Independent clause

6 Independent clause

7 Dependent clause

8 Independent clause

9 Independent clause

10 Dependent clause

Exercise 6

1. The pizza finally arrived, **but** they got our order wrong!

2. I can't swim well, **so** I stay in the shallow end.

3. I went home **since** the rain wouldn't let up.

> Sentences 1 and 6 can use *and* or *but*.

4. She didn't try the shrimp, **nor** did she try the oysters.

5. The Ferris wheel was stuck, **yet** the brave children were not afraid.

6. Frank bought a hot dog **and** Matilda bought a vanilla shake.

7. We can go to the concert **or** we can stay home.

8. Richie's mother was shocked, **for** Richie had dyed his hair blue.

Exercise 7

> Answers may vary. Your answer is correct if:
> - It has an independent clause and a dependent clause.
> - The word you circled is a coordinating conjunction.

1. We drove to the airport safely, (even) in the snow.

2. We brought binoculars (because) we are birdwatching.

3. I will go to the party with you (if) you wake me up.

4. (When) she fell off the chair, her cheeks flushed.

5. She started to believe in ghosts (as) she got older.

6. (Despite) my allergy, I love to eat chocolate!

Exercise 8

Answers will vary. Your answers are correct if:

- All your sentences express a complete idea and make sense.
- Your simple sentence has a subject and a verb.
- Your complex sentence has an independent clause and a dependent clause.
- Your compound sentence has two independent clauses.
- Your compound complex sentence has two independent clauses and a dependent clause.
- You use conjunctions to connect clauses.

Sample answers:

1. simple: I have freckles on my nose.
   subject — I; *verb* — have

2. complex: Because I have freckles on my nose, I look like my mom.
   conjunction — Because; *dependent clause* — I have freckles on my nose; *independent clause* — I look like my mom.

3. compound: I have freckles on my nose, but I don't have any on my face.
   independent clause #1 — I have freckles on my nose; *conjunction* — but; *independent clause #2* — I don't have any on my face.

4. compound complex: I have freckles on my nose, but I don't have any on my face, even though my mom does.
   independent clause #1 — I have freckles on my nose; *conjunction* — but; *independent clause #2* — I don't have any on my face; *conjunction* — even though; *dependent clause* — my mom does.

Exercise 9

Answers may vary. To check if your new sentence is correct, ask yourself:

- What is the modifier?
- What does it describe?
- Is it clear what the modifier describes?
- Does the sentence make sense?

1. Fumbling in her backpack, the wallet was not found. → *dangling*

   Fumbling in her backpack, she could not find the wallet.

2 (Melting in the sun) made the table sticky.

The popsicle melting in the sun made the table sticky.

misplaced

3 The waiter served a steak to the guest that was too rare.

The waiter served the guest a steak that was too rare.

4 Crying in the emergency room, the nurse stitched Keith's wound.

The nurse stitched Keith's wound as he was crying in the emergency room.

5 The tourist bought a crepe from the friendly vendor covered in powdered sugar.

The tourist bought a crepe covered in powdered sugar from the friendly vendor.

6 (Expecting a meteor shower,) the telescope was positioned correctly.

Expecting a meteor shower, Min positioned the telescope correctly.

7 (Driving to the party) the cake tilted dangerously in the passenger seat.

Driving to the party, the baker noticed the cake tilt dangerously in the passenger seat.

8 Kristina saw a black cat on her way to the Halloween party.

On her way to the Halloween party, Kristina saw a black cat.

9 My parents bought a parrot for my sister <u>with big red feathers</u>.

My parents bought a parrot <u>with big red feathers</u> for my sister.

10 Elaine walked the poodle <u>wearing her prom dress</u>.

<u>Wearing her prom dress</u>, Elaine walked the poodle.

Exercise 10

incomplete sentence

<u>On the first day of summer vacation.</u> I was excited to relax and unwind

dangling modifier

at the beach with my family. <u>Ate breakfast quickly</u> and dashed to the car.

incomplete sentence   *dangling modifier*

<u>Ready to go!</u> <u>Riding along in the back seat, the beach suddenly came into

view.</u> I couldn't wait to sink my toes into the sand. We carried all the

beach gear to our spot, I was finally able to relax. I closed my eyes and lis-

misplaced modifier

tened as seagulls squawked overhead. <u>Crashing on the shore,</u> I could hear

wrong conjunction

the waves. The sun's rays felt warm on my skin. A gentle breeze blew <u>since</u>

ruffled my hair. Next to me, my brother and dad planned their sandcastle.

needs a conjunction

<u>We arrived at the beach early, the sandcastle could be gigantic!</u>

Answers will vary. Your paragraph is correct if:
- It adds subjects for all dangling modifiers.
- It clarifies the subject of misplaced modifiers.
- All sentences express complete ideas.
- Sentences include the correct conjunctions when needed.

Sample answer:

On the first day of summer vacation, I was excited to relax and unwind at the beach with my family. We ate breakfast quickly and dashed to the car. We were ready to go! As I rode along in the back seat, the beach suddenly came into view. I couldn't wait to sink my toes in the sand. After we carried all the beach gear to our spot, I was finally able to relax. I closed my eyes and listened as seagulls squawked overhead. I could hear the waves crashing on the shore. The sun's rays felt warm on my skin. A gentle breeze blew and ruffled my hair. Next to me, my brother and dad planned their sandcastle. Since we arrived at the beach early, the sandcastle could be gigantic!

CHAPTER 2: PRONOUNS

Exercise 1

Last week, I finally got a dog! Convincing my parents was not an easy task. It took strong persuasive skills. My mother is allergic to animals. When she is near them, she sneezes and her eyes get itchy. Sometimes she even breaks out in hives! My father, on the other hand, was worried a dog would scratch up the hardwood floors or ruin his favorite sneakers. He also argued that owning a dog is a large responsibility. "Are you going to walk it every day?" he asked. "Who is going to pick up the poop? I myself will absolutely not!"

Nobody thought I had a chance, but I came up with a clever plan. For weeks, I helped with lots of chores to show my parents I am responsible. I hid pictures of adorable Goldendoodle puppies everywhere, even under their pillows! Who could resist those soft brown eyes, tiny paws, and fluffy tails? To everyone's surprise, my parents relented. Overjoyed, I named our new dog Viking. She is the cutest dog in the whole world! We love her very much.

1. Subjective pronouns: I, she, he, who, we

2. Reflexive pronouns: myself

3. Possessive pronouns: his, her, my, our, their

4. Indefinite pronouns: nobody, everywhere, everyone

Exercise 2

subject → object

1 Jacob cut the grass.

2 The lifeguard rescued the drowning swimmer.

3 For dessert, I picked a king-size candy bar.

4 Phineas ate the cheeseburger, even though it was cold.

5 The tornado destroyed the home in five seconds flat.

6 My teacher took attendance.

7 The van pulled into the parking lot.

8 She decorated the cupcakes with purple icing.

9 The chef grilled the lamb chops.

10 We could not connect to the internet.

Exercise 3

1 S
  I bought some new ballet shoes.

2 S   O
  I never said we would bake a cake for the party.

3   S
  Together, they ate pancakes for dinner.

4 S   O
  You can join us on the dance floor!

5 S   O
  I didn't see him digging up the rosebush!

6   S
  Is it possible to take the test again?

7 She said the spending limit is twenty bucks.

S

8 Do you know who sent the package?

S   O

Exercise 4

Answers will vary. To check yours, ask yourself:
- What noun is the pronoun replacing?
- Is that noun singular or plural?

Sample answers:

1 Singular
Jamar waited for me at the bus stop.

2 Singular or plural
You will be late to school if you don't leave right now.

3 Singular or plural
They always play pickleball on Saturday.

4 Singular
I have always excelled in math.

5 Plural
We would be delighted to show you around town.

6 Singular or plural
The boy scout badges are theirs.

7 Singular
Her name was passed down to her grandchild.

8 Plural
Daphne invited us to play mini golf.

Exercise 5

1. <u>Everyone</u> was able to complete the marathon.

2. Are all these gifts for <u>you</u>?

3. <u>Nobody</u> could believe it was snowing in July.

4. <u>Who</u> gave you that cool hat?

5. <u>What</u> happened to the rug?

6. Connor is eating his jelly beans now, but I'll eat <u>mine</u> later.

7. The diamond lost <u>its</u> shine.

8. Don't tell <u>me</u> what to do!

9. <u>They</u> got caught in the rain on their run.

10. Everyone forgot it was <u>his</u> birthday.

Exercise 6

1. I found <u>myself</u> thinking about the past more than ever.

2. They found the buried treasure hidden on the island all by <u>themselves</u>.

3. You need to do the math homework <u>yourself</u>. ⟵ or yourselves

4. The acrobat practiced the routine by <u>himself</u> several times a week. ⟵ or herself

5. We baked the birthday cake <u>ourselves</u>.

6. The bathrooms are new, but the school <u>itself</u> was built more than 100 years ago.

or himself

7   The chef created the extensive menu <u>herself</u>.

or yourself

8   You got <u>yourselves</u> into this mess, so you have to get <u>yourselves</u> out!

Exercise 7

1   **They** went to the grocery store. Wrong case

2   I'm going to bring **her** along for the ride. Wrong case

3   I want to ride the roller coaster alone. C

4   Every time I eat pizza, **I** get pepperoni on it. Wrong number

5   She can't wait to see them at the cookout. C

6   The customer didn't know what they wanted. C

7   Help **me** pack my suitcase, please. Wrong case

8   If you need an extra pillow, **you** should ask. Wrong number

9   When I go to the movies, I get popcorn with extra butter. C

10   **I** found a giant rubber duck in the bathtub. Wrong case

Exercise 8

1   Incorrect
Jooahn and **I** are taking the bus.

2   Correct
<u>The librarian and I</u> recommend the book *Camp QUILTBAG* by Nicole Melleby and A. J. Sass.

3   Incorrect
The haunted house scared **me and Shaquana** so badly, we screamed at the top of our lungs!

4 Correct

It's time for <u>me and him</u> to hit the hay.

5 Incorrect

Even though we are teenagers, Lisseth and I refuse
to believe that Santa Claus isn't real.

BONUS QUESTION: Inappropraite shifts! The cases don't match.

Exercise 9

1 He and Constance will present the award for best dressed.

2 My father and I sat front row at the World Series this year.

3 If they and Paula can solve the equation,
our team will win the tournament.

4 Give the magazines to us and Fanny.

5 He and Carlos got lost on the first day of school.

6 Kristos and I will catch the runaway chickens!

7 We and the campers can pitch the tents.

8 There were enough blankets for the family and me.

9 Abe and I will do all the laundry.

10 She and her friends formed a mystery-solving club.

CHAPTER 3: ACTIVE AND PASSIVE VOICE

Exercise 1

1. Serita <u>uploaded</u> the video to her Snapchat story.   Active

2. Piping-hot potato latkes <u>were served</u> by my mother.   Passive

3. Diwali <u>was celebrated</u> by my family with fireworks,   Passive
   feasts, and fancy outfits!

4. Colin <u>tickled</u> his little sister.   Active

5. The red envelopes <u>were given</u> to the children on Lunar New Year.   Passive

6. Mrs. Phillips <u>collected</u> the algebra tests at exactly two o'clock.   Active

7. The pot of jjamppong <u>was devoured</u> by Mrs. Liú's guests.   Passive

8. Jae <u>read</u> six volumes of their favorite manga series in one night!   Active

Exercise 2

1. The detective secured the crime scene.

2. The toddler ate a snickerdoodle.

3. Superman captured Lex Luthor.

4. The artist tattooed a flower on Jasmine's arm.

5. Kennedy used a selfie stick to take the picture.

6. A fire damaged the Notre-Dame cathedral.

7. James's dad invited Connie and Hunter to the birthday party.

8. Jonas explored the art museum for hours.

> Answers may vary. If you can say "yes" to the following questions, your sentence is in active voice.
> - Is the subject of my sentence doing the action?
> - Does my sentence make sense?

9 The quarterback led the team to victory.

10 The principal reprimanded the rowdy students.

The Hunger Games <u>was written by Suzanne Collins</u>. This dystopian book <u>is enjoyed by young adults</u> all around the world. In *The Hunger Games*, a nation of twelve districts, called Panem, <u>is controlled by the Capitol</u>. Each year, twenty-four district children <u>are forced by the Capitol to compete</u> in an event called the Hunger Games, where they fight to the death until only one is left standing. A lottery selects which kids will fight.

District 12 <u>is lived in by the protagonist</u>, Katniss Everdeen. When her younger sister, Prim, <u>is selected by the lottery</u> as tribute, Katniss volunteers to take her place. That year the baker's son Peeta <u>is also chosen by the lottery</u>. Katniss and Peeta <u>are escorted to the Capitol by chaperones</u>.

Before the Hunger Games begin, all the tributes train. As they train, the tributes <u>are observed by game makers</u> who want to assess their strengths and weaknesses. Tributes <u>are also interviewed by Caesar Flickerman</u> on national television. If a tribute's interview goes well, gifts from generous viewers <u>might be sent to them</u> to help them survive. When the games begin Katniss, Peeta, and the other tributes <u>are tested by a series of life-threatening obstacles</u>.

The light of day <u>will only be seen by one winner</u>.

Check the sentences in your rewritten passage by asking yourself:
Does the subject of this sentence do the action?

Suzanne Collins wrote *The Hunger Games*. Young adults around the world enjoy this dystopian book. In *The Hunger Games*, the Capitol controls a nation of twelve districts called Panem. The protagonist Katniss Everdeen lives in District 12. Each year, the Capitol forces twenty-four district children to compete in an event called the Hunger Games, where they fight to the death until only one is left standing. A lottery selects which kids will fight.

The protagonist, Katniss Everdeen, lives in District 12. When the lottery selects her younger sister, Prim, as tribute, Katniss volunteers to take her place. That year, the lottery also selects Peeta, the baker's son. Chaperones escort Katniss and Peeta to the Capitol.

Before the Hunger Games begin, all the tributes train. Game makers observe them as they train, to assess their strengths and weaknesses. Caesar Flickerman also interviews the tributes on national television. If a tribute's interview goes well, generous viewers might send them gifts to help them survive. When the games begin, a series of life-threatening obstacles test Katniss, Peeta, and the other tributes.

Only one winner will see the light of day.

Exercise 4

1. **Future tense:** Drew <u>will host</u> the baby shower.
   Voice: active voice

2. **Present tense:** The Oscar-winning film <u>is produced</u> by a brand-new studio.
   Voice: passive voice

3. **Past tense:** Keyrin <u>passed</u> the naan around the table.
   Voice: active voice

4. **Past tense:** This pizzeria <u>made</u> more than ten specialty pies.
   Voice: active voice

5. **Future tense:** The St. Patrick's Day parade <u>will be</u> so much fun.
   Voice: active voice

6. **Present tense:** Chicken empanadas <u>are served</u> by the food truck.
   Voice: passive voice

Exercise 5

1. The cars were washed by the football team to raise money for new equipment.

2. The hoodie was worn by Sheila even though it was 90 degrees out.

3. Five new science fiction books were ordered by Marius to read on vacation.

4. Paint was spilled on the brand-new living room rug by the five-year-old.

5. Three burgers and three strawberry shakes were delivered to our table by the server.

6. A careless mistake was made on the exam by the student.

7. Three more melting glaciers in Antarctica have been discovered by scientists.

8. The tray of lasagna was devoured by the volleyball team after practice.

9. The national anthem was sung by Beyoncé at the Super Bowl.

10. Four dozen apple pies were donated by the bakery to the camp.

BONUS QUESTION: You might observe that the sentences written in passive voice are weaker. They are more wordy, less straightforward, and don't sound as polished.

Exercise 6

1 Passive

The artist scrawled graffiti all over the building.

2 Passive

The students finally elected their class president.

3 Passive

After dinner, we cleaned and put away the dishes in the sink.

4 Active

5 Passive

Monica wore a rainbow bandana.

6 Active

7 Passive

Humans should always protect endangered species.

8 Active

> Check if your new sentences are in active voice by asking: Does the subject of the sentence do the action?

CHAPTER 4: VERBS AND MOOD

Exercise 1

1 D

2 A

3 E

4 G

5 B

6 F

7 C

Exercise 2

PRESENT	PAST	FUTURE
1 I fly	I flew	I will fly
2 You gloat	You gloated	You will gloat
3 They clip	They clipped	They will clip
4 He skips	He skipped	He will skip
5 I stop	I stopped	I will stop
6 You climb	You climbed	You will climb
7 She teases	She teased	She will tease
8 I observe	I observed	I will observe
9 We shovel	We shoveled	We will shovel
10 I rock	I rocked	I will rock

Exercise 3

1 Interrogative

2 Imperative

3 Indicative

4 Interrogative

5 Subjunctive

6 Conditional

7 Conditional

8 Imperative

9 Subjunctive

10 Indicative

Exercise 4

1. **Indicative:** I like to go ice skating.
   Imperative: Go ice skating with me!
   Interrogative: Do you like to go ice skating?

2. **Indicative:** He is in the way.
   Imperative: Get out of the way!
   Interrogative: Am I in the way?

   Answers will vary. Check your answers by asking these questions:
   - Does my indicative sentence make a statement?
   - Does my imperative sentence give a command or direction?
   - Does my interrogative sentence ask a question?

3. **Indicative:** This is Lauren's bed.
   Imperative: Get in bed, Lauren!
   Interrogative: Is this Lauren's bed?

4. **Indicative:** I shut the television off.
   Imperative: Shut the television off!
   Interrogative: Did I shut the television off?

5. **Indicative:** I went shopping.
   Imperative: Go shopping!
   Interrogative: Can I go shopping?

6. **Indicative:** I eat dinner.
   Imperative: Eat your dinner!
   Interrogative: Did you eat your dinner?

7. **Indicative:** Susan slowed down.
   Imperative: Slow down, Susan!
   Interrogative: Did Susan slow down?

8. **Indicative:** Miriam tied her shoes.
   Imperative: Miriam, tie your shoes!
   Interrogative: Did Miriam tie her shoes?

9 **Indicative:** Violet uses her calculator for math homework.
Imperative: Violet, use your calculator for math homework.
Interrogative: Violet, did you use your calculator for math homework?

10 **Indicative:** You rested after the trip.
Imperative: Rest after your trip!
Interrogative: Did you rest after the trip?

Exercise 5

1 If I jump, that shark will bite me! C ← C for conditional

2 They would be a great babysitter if they liked kids. C

3 If you get home past midnight, you will turn into a pumpkin! S ←
S for subjunctive

4 I would speak Italian better if I practiced regularly. C

5 If you leave me alone with this chocolate cake, there won't be any left when you get back! C

6 I wish I could snap my fingers and shape-shift into a bird. S

7 If I had every Pokémon card in print, my collection would be valuable. C

8 If I had a time machine, I would visit the Jurassic Period and ride a stegosaurus! S

Exercise 6

Sample answer:

MY ROLE MODEL IS: Simone Biles

Verb Mood	Sentence
Indicative	Simone Biles is an Olympian.
Imperative	Make sure you watch Simone Biles perform tonight.
Interrogative	Did you know Simone Biles led the U.S. women's gymnastics team at the Rio Olympics?
Conditional	If I won a gold medal at the Olympics, like Simone Biles, my parents would be very proud.
Subjunctive	If I could be Simone Biles for a day, I would land a triple-double!

CHAPTER 5: VERBALS

Exercise 1

1 B

2 I

3 D

4 A

5 C

6 G

7 E

8 F

9 H

10 J

Exercise 2

1 Exercising is good for your body and mind.

2 I love baking pecan pies on Thanksgiving!

3 You might be sorry, but apologizing is not enough this time.

4 At the assembly, students learned that vaping is dangerous.

5 When she got caught, Laurie realized that cheating is not the answer.

6 Now that she is in high school, Chloe is trying to improve her grades

7 Would you mind training my dog to do tricks?

8 While abroad, we noticed that speaking multiple languages is helpful.

9 Keke knew that memorizing her lines would be difficult.

10 Practicing your card tricks makes you a better magician.

Exercise 3

Answers will vary. If you can answer "yes" to these three questions, your answer is correct!

- Does my gerund end in -ing?
- Does my gerund or gerund phrase act like a noun?
- Does the sentence make sense?

Sample answers:

1   My favorite winter activity is <u>snowboarding</u>.

Or skiing, or having snowball fights!

2   <u>Eating</u> too many gummy bears in one sitting can give you a stomachache.

3   <u>Seeing</u> fireworks on the Fourth of July is exciting!

4   When you pay attention in class, <u>getting</u> good grades is not as hard as you think.

5   <u>Studying</u> a little each day helped the students ace their tests.

6   <u>Speaking</u> in front of a crowd can be terrifying!

7   This summer vacation, <u>learning</u> to juggle five balls at once is Shanae's goal.

8   <u>Looking both ways</u> before you cross the street can keep you safe.

9   If you have a problem, <u>talking about it</u> with your friends can help.

10   <u>Waiting in line</u> at the amusement park is boring!

Exercise 4

1 Singing in the shower is a great way to start the morning.

2 Luca hates mowing the lawn.

3 Playing Candy Crush can be addictive.

The gerunds in questions 2, 5, 7, and 9, are NOT the subject of the sentence!

4 Reading is my favorite rainy-day activity.

5 Why don't you like fishing?

6 Finding a lost hamster in your house can be tricky!

7 They like listening to K-pop when they clean their room.

8 Painting is harder than it looks!

9 I'm too tired to go hiking today.

10 Making friends in a new school takes time.

Exercise 5

1 Aaliyah's tattered scarf is falling apart. Present

If you're having a hard time telling the difference between past and present participles, remember: Present participles end in -ing!

2 Jada kept the crew waiting. Present

3 Terrence looked worried when he started the pop quiz. Past

4 When the car hit the curb, the front tire was damaged. Past

5 We felt exhausted after the long plane ride. Past

6 Tony's plan seems confusing. Present

7 Nova was invited to the party, but she didn't want to go. Past

8 The frozen pond was perfect for <u>playing</u> hockey.   *Present*

9 The <u>burnt</u> toast was inedible.   *Past*

10 The substitute was <u>fired</u> because he fell asleep on the job!   *Past*

Exercise 6

Sample answers:

Answers will vary. To check if your sentence is correct, ask yourself:
- Does the past participle modify a noun?
- What noun does it modify?
- Does the sentence make sense?

1 Bake
The half-baked loaf of bread was still gooey in the middle.

2 Ruin
The baker stared at the ruined cake.

3 Find
I have found the secret passage!

4 Haunt
Claire was convinced the barn was haunted.

5 Sauté
I prefer the chicken sautéed.

6 Break
They say he died of a broken heart.

7 Write
Sam has written an impressive poem.

8 Take
You have taken the wrong path.

Exercise 7

modifies

1 Listening to the radio, Uncle Al fell asleep.

2 The chicken roasting in the oven smelled delicious.

> If it's hard to tell what the participle phrase modifies, ask yourself: What noun does it describe or give more information about?

3 The man searching the mansion can't find his diamond earring.

4 The girl wearing purple Crocs is my cousin.

5 The couple walking along the beach held hands.

6 Ripped at the knee, the jeans were old.

7 Glazed with icing, the cinnamon buns cooled.

8 Shouting with happiness, the children opened their gifts.

Exercise 8

1 Gerund phrase

2 Present participle phrase

> Both of these verbals end in –ing, but a gerund phrase acts as a noun, while a present participle phrase acts as an adjective.

3 Gerund phrase

4 Present participle phrase

5 Present participle phrase

6 Gerund phrase

7 Present participle phrase

8 Gerund phrase

9 Present participle phrase

10 Gerund phrase

Exercise 9

Sample answers:

Or "to try" or "to start!"

1 Saul was eager <u>to go</u> surfing.

2 I am learning <u>to make</u> macaroons.

3 Alicia was ready <u>to move</u> to the city.

4 Diego offered <u>to bring</u> the dessert.

5 Jules likes <u>to study</u> by herself.

6 The students were amazed <u>to discover</u> a pupa in the praying mantis's tank.

7 The acrobats were trying <u>to rehearse</u> a new routine.

8 My auntie taught me how <u>to ride</u> a bike.

9 Crystal put on her coat <u>to take</u> a walk.

10 Abuela hopes <u>to visit</u> us over the summer.

> Answers will vary. If you can answer "yes" to these questions, your answer is correct!
> - Does the infinitive start with "to"?
> - Does the infinitive end with a verb?
> - Does the sentence make sense?

Exercise 10

1 Would you like to work together? noun

2 The actors were ready to rehearse the death scene. adverb

3 To become a member of the National Honor Society, you must get good grades. adverb

4 In my family it is tradition to make ravioli on Christmas. adjective

5 Do you have the motivation to train for a marathon? adjective

6 Madison wants to build the set for the play. noun

7 The athletes were thrilled to make the playoffs. adverb

8 Ramneet's chore is to take out the trash. noun

9 The group got tickets to see the circus. adjective

10 Tricia needed someone to feed her fish when she was at camp. adjective

CHAPTER 6: DEFINING FROM CONTEXT

Exercise 1

1 B

2 C

3 A

4 B

5 C

6 B

7 D

8 A

9 D

10 B

Exercise 2

1. "Incentive" means something that motivates us to do something.

   If parents gave their children an allowance at the end of the week, children would have an incentive to help around the house.

2. "Trepidation" means fear in anticipation of something happening.

   Jenna approached the roller coaster with trepidation after hearing screams of terror from other riders.

3. "Lofty" means giant or high.

   Pauline met her parents' lofty expectations by excelling in all her classes, mastering trombone and piano, starring in the winter musical, and running for class president.

4. "Mediate" means to help end a dispute between other people.

   After Suzanne mediated a fight between her two best friends, everyone enjoyed going out for ice cream together.

5. "Lucrative" means producing a lot of money or a profit.

   The tennis team's lucrative after-school bake sale raised enough money to replace thirty rackets for the upcoming season.

6. "Loathe" means to strongly dislike or be disgusted by.

   Theresa loathes cheese because it smells stinky and gives her a terrible stomachache.

7. "Adept" means very skilled.

   Ling, an adept mah-jongg player, has learned many helpful strategies from her grandmother.

8 "Fabricate" means to make something up.

When Mrs. Breen questioned Phil about his tardiness, he quickly fabricated an elaborate excuse.

9 "Boisterous" means noisy and energetic.

The boisterous crowd stomped their feet and chanted Serena Williams's name as she emerged on the court.

10 "Flaunt" means to show something off to other people to make them jealous.

As Molly flaunted her new Gucci bag, her friends and frenemies stared enviously.

Exercise 3

Sample answers:

1 It is hard to plan a beach day when the weather is so erratic.

2 This mentoring program helps teens flourish in school.

3 When Darren's last final exam ended, he immediately felt his stress abate.

4 Carefully wrapping leftover pizza in aluminum foil can increase its longevity in the freezer.

5 At first the villagers were nervous around the giant, but in time they learned he was benign.

6 The invaders' plot to usurp the throne was unsuccessful.

7 Jessica used to be very popular, but her haughty attitude cost her some friends.

> Answers will vary. To check if your sentences are correct, ask yourself these questions:
> - Does it use the word correctly?
> - Does it provide at least one clue to help a reader know the definition of the word?
> - Does my sentence make sense?

8 It was annoying listening to Mitch brag about his affluent lifestyle.

9 Fortunately, Ang's long hair did not obstruct his vision while he played violin.

10 Mom's terse reply made it clear she was in a terrible mood.

Exercise 4

1 **Renowned** Famous or known by a lot of people
   synonym: Esteemed, celebrated, acclaimed

2 **Advocate** Someone who publicly supports a cause
   synonym: Supporter, champion, proponent

3 **Cognizant** Being aware of something
   synonym: Conscious, aware, mindful

4 **Adamant** Stubborn, refusing to change one's mind
   synonym: Determined, steadfast

5 **Initiative** A new plan or process to achieve a goal
   synonym: Ambition, action, drive

6 **Fervent** Displaying a passionate intensity
   synonym: Impassioned, intense, heartfelt

Exercise 5

Answers will vary. Check your answers against the definition in a dictionary.

CHAPTER 7: AFFIXES AND ROOTS

Exercise 1

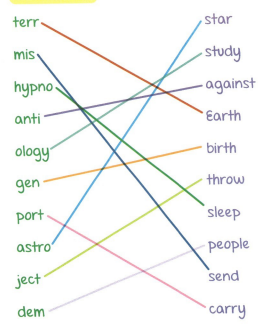

terr · · star
mis · · study
hypno · · against
anti · · Earth
ology · · birth
gen · · throw
port · · sleep
astro · · people
ject · · send
dem · · carry

Exercise 2

Answers may vary. Sample answers:

1. Astro: astrology, astronomical, astrolabe

2. Ject: inject, object, reject

3. Ology: anthropology, biology, sociology

4. Port: important, deport, export

5. Mis: mission, transmission, promise

6. Magni: magnificent, magnitude, magnanimous

7. Scope: kaleidoscope, horoscope, microscopic

8 Dem: demographic, pandemic, epidemic

9 Phobos: hydrophobic, arachnophobia, xenophobic, homophobic

10 Chron: chronicle, chronic, synchronized

11 Cycl: cycle, cyclops, recycle, unicycle

12 Geo: geology, geothermal, geopolitics

13 Hydro: hydrate, hydrant, hydroplane, hydraulic

14 Mech: machinery, mechanic, mechanical

15 Phon: megaphone, microphone, homophone, cacophony, symphony

Exercise 3

Sample answers:

1 Words using the suffix -ful:

Careful	Joyful
Mouthful	Painful
Shameful	Willful
Lawful	

> Answers will vary. To check if your answers are correct, ask yourself:
> • Does the suffix come at the end of the word? Is the word in the dictionary?
> • Does the prefix come at the beginning of the word? Is the word in the dictionary?

All of these words express a lot of something (a lot of joy, or a lot of pain).

The suffix -ful means full of something or having the qualities of something.

2 Words using the prefix re-:

Repeat	Remember
Revise	Rewire
Replay	Regret
Reload	

All of these words mean doing something again.

The prefix re- means again or back.

3 <u>Biology</u>: "Bio" means life, so biology means the study of life.

   <u>Geology</u>: "Geo" means earth, so geology means the study of earth.

   <u>Dermatology</u>: "Derma" means skin, so dermatology means the study of skin.

   <u>Psychology</u>: "Psych" means mind, so psychology means the study of the mind.

Exercise 4

1 <u>Triangle</u> a shape with three angles

2 <u>Unwind</u> to undo after being wound

3 <u>Abandonment</u> the act of leaving something or someone

4 <u>Portable</u> able to be carried, or transported

5 <u>Preview</u> a look at something beforehand

6 <u>Encouragement</u> the act of giving someone support, confidence, or hope

7 <u>Colorful</u> having lots of colors, or full of interest

8 <u>Cheerless</u> unpleasant or sad; without cheer

9 <u>Reliable</u> consistent or able to be trusted

10 <u>Unhappy</u> not satisfied or pleased

Exercise 5

1. <u>Disadvantage</u> Prefix
2. <u>Companion</u> Prefix
3. <u>Preventable</u> Suffix
4. <u>Improper</u> Prefix
5. <u>Rewrite</u> Prefix
6. <u>Nonsense</u> Prefix
7. <u>Cardiac</u> Suffix
8. <u>Premade</u> Prefix
9. <u>Unkind</u> Prefix
10. <u>Helpless</u> Suffix

Exercise 6

Do you ever procrastinate before starting a task? Many people struggle with deadlines, so chances are you probably have. Perhaps you've waited until the night before a project was due to start working on it. Delaying progress on an unenjoyable task is a common problem for teenagers and adults alike. Studies have proven that procrastination can produce a great deal of anxiety and stress. Research also shows that procrastination can be "particularly pronounced in students" (Cherry 2022). *Psychological Bulletin* found that a whopping 80% to 95% of college students procrastinate on a regular basis (Steel 2007), particularly when it comes to completing assignments and coursework. Experts offer promising advice: To promote productivity and avoid getting off task, it helps to be proactive. Before you proceed, eliminate distractions and set goals. This process may prove to help you keep your promises!

1. Pro

2. To move to a higher position or rank.

3. Pro means to move forward.

Exercise 7

1. <u>Aquarium</u>: Aqua means water.

2. <u>Circumference</u>: Circum means around or surrounding.

3. <u>Malignant</u>: Mal means bad.

   Aqua is also a root. It means water!
4. <u>Aquaphobia</u>: Phobia means an extreme fear of something.

5. <u>Dictionary</u>: Dict means say.

6. <u>Factory</u>: Fact means made.

7. <u>Pesticide</u>: Cide means to kill.

   Therm is also a root. It means heat! What does a thermometer do?
8. <u>Thermometer</u>: Meter means measure.

9. <u>Monologue</u>: Mono means one.

   Bio and graphy are also roots! Bio means life and graphy means writing.
10. <u>Autobiography</u>: Auto means self.

Exercise 1

> Answers will vary. If your synonyms are listed in the thesaurus for each word below, then your answer is correct. Great job!

1	Evil	immoral	base	vile
2	Skill	expertise	dexterity	prowess
3	Powerful	mighty	dominant	influential
4	Thoughtful	pensive	introspective	contemplative
5	Rude	impudent	insolent	impertinent
6	Sneaky	conniving	devious	duplicitous
7	Enthusiastic	keen	fervent	ardent
8	Lonely	isolated	solitary	reclusive
9	Stinky	noxious	putrid	revolting
10	Hard	strenuous	arduous	grueling

Exercise 2

1 True

2 False   If you want to find the definition of terms used in your biology textbook, you should use a glossary or dictionary.

3 True

4 True

5 False <u>Some</u> words have only one syllable, <u>but most</u> <u>words have more than one syllable.</u>

6 True

7 False You see \'kər-nəl\ next to the word "colonel." This tells you the word's <u>pronunciation</u>.

8 False A glossary usually appears at the <u>end</u> of a text.

9 False A pronunciation guide tells you <u>how to pronounce a</u> <u>word</u>. A dictionary might tell you a word's <u>origin</u>.

10 True

Exercise 3

1 Dictionary

2 Dictionary (the pronunciation guide!)

3 Glossary

4 Dictionary

5 Thesaurus

6 Dictionary

7 Thesaurus

8 Dictionary (the pronunciation guide!)

9 Glossary

10 Thesaurus

Exercise 4

Entry Word

Syllables

Part of Speech

Pronunciation

Definition

Example sentence

Part of Speech

Definition

mutiny *(noun)* mu·ti·ny | \'myü-tə-nē\ : forcible or passive resistance to lawful authority *especially*: concerted revolt (as of a naval crew) against discipline or a superior officer *The sailors staged a **mutiny** and took control of the ship.*

(verb) : to rise against or refuse to obey or observe authority

entry word

part of speech

syllables

pronunciation guide

definition (1)

conscientious *(adjective)* con·sci·en·tious | \ˌkän(t)-shē-'en(t)-shəs\ **1**: meticulous, careful **2**: governed by or conforming to the dictates of conscience: scrupulous

*He was a **conscientious** public servant.*

example sentence

definition (2)

entry word

part of speech

syllables

pronunciation guide

definition

despondent *(adjective)* de·spon·dent | \di-'spän-dənt\ : feeling or showing extreme discouragement, dejection, or depression *He was **despondent** about his health.*

example sentence

354

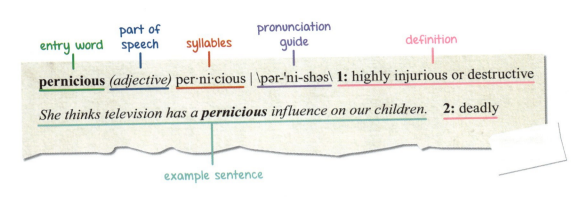

entry word · part of speech · syllables · pronunciation guide · definition

pernicious *(adjective)* per·ni·cious | \pər-'ni-shəs\ **1:** highly injurious or destructive

*She thinks television has a **pernicious** influence on our children.* **2:** deadly

example sentence

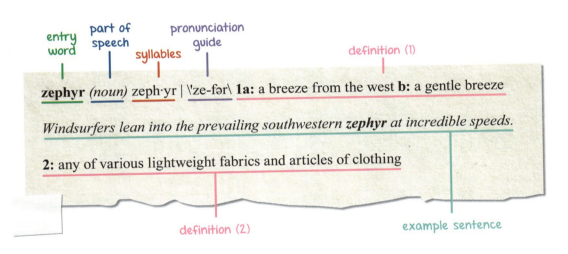

entry word · part of speech · syllables · pronunciation guide · definition (1)

zephyr *(noun)* zeph·yr | \'ze-fər\ **1a:** a breeze from the west **b:** a gentle breeze

*Windsurfers lean into the prevailing southwestern **zephyr** at incredible speeds.*

2: any of various lightweight fabrics and articles of clothing

definition (2) · example sentence

Exercise 5

1 The Merriam-Webster online dictionary has
   several definitions of the word "apex":

   > 1. the uppermost point
   > 2. the highest or culminating point
   > 3. the point of the sharpest curvature in a path
   >   (such as that followed by a turning vehicle)

2 The Merriam-Webster dictionary provides two definitions for the word "erratic":

   > 1. having no fixed course : wandering
   > 2. characterized by a lack of consistency, regularity, or uniformity

3 The word "exacerbate" is a verb. It means to
   make worse or increase the severity.

4 The noun form of "exacerbate" is "exacerbating."

5 ˌig-nə-ˈmi-nē-əs.

6 According to the Merriam-Webster dictionary, "ignominious" has five syllables:

   > ig • no • min • i • ous
   > 1   2   3   4   5

7 According to the Merriam-Webster dictionary,
   there are two definitions for "petulant":

   > 1. insolent or rude in speech or behavior
   > 2. characterized by temporary or capricious ill humor; peevish

8 The dictionary provides this example sentence for "petulant":
   He was often moody and petulant.

9 Answers will vary. Sample: When Gina was in middle
   school, she often came home in a petulant mood.

10 According to the dictionary, the plural form of "curriculum" is "curricula."

Exercise 6

1 B

2 B

3 B

4 A

5 A

6 B

7 A

8 B

9 A

10 A

Exercise 7

1 **Homely:** not elaborate or complex

2 **Solicit:** to request urgently or persistently

3 **Succinctly:** marked by compact, precise words

4 **Expound:** to explain by setting forth in careful and often elaborate detail

5 **Phantasm:** something existing in perception only

6 **Docility:** the state of being easily managed or handled; ready to accept control or instruction; submissive

7 **Disposition:** the predominant or prevailing tendency of one's spirits; natural mental and emotional outlook or mood; characteristic attitude

8 **Sagacious:** acutely insightful and wise

9 **Derivable:** taken from a specified source

10 **Paltry:** inferior, meager

Exercise 8

baffle
banter
beckon
beguile
bequeath
blaze
boisterous
bravado
burgeon
bygone

observant
occur
oodles
optimistic
original
originate
ornament
otherworldly
overflow
outfox

UNIT 2
Language

Exercise 1

Sample answers:

1. Tina has a <u>heart of stone</u>. ← idiom

2. Reading the textbook <u>bored me to death</u>. ↖ hyperbole

> Answers will vary. If your sentence is correct, it will:
> - Use at least one type of figurative language: idiom, metaphor, simile, allusion, personification, pun, hyperbole, or onomatopoeia.
> - Express the same meaning as the original sentence.
> - Make sense!

3. When Julissa heard the bad news, <u>her head spun like a top</u>. ↖ simile

4. I am so tired <u>I could sleep for 100 years</u>. ↖ hyperbole

5. The raindrops <u>plunked</u>, <u>plopped</u>, and <u>pattered</u> ← onomatopoeia on the tin roof.

6. When we saw the painting, we all agreed: Todd <u>is a modern-day Picasso</u>. ↖ allusion

Exercise 2

1. Simile
2. Metaphor
3. Metaphor
4. Simile
5. Metaphor
6. Simile

Exercise 3

1. Personification
2. Allusion
3. Hyperbole
4. Personification
5. Idiom
6. Pun
7. Hyperbole
8. Onomatopoeia

Exercise 4

Sample answers:

Answers will vary. Your sentence is correct if it:
- Gives the inanimate subject a human behavior or characteristic.
- Makes sense!

1. The stream sang a cheerful tune.

2. The stars winked down at me.

3. The breeze nudged me through the door.

4. The shoes fought against my feet.

5. The train wheezed around the bend.

Exercise 5

Answers will vary. Your sentence is correct if it:
- Uses a word that sounds like what it describes.
- Makes sense!

Sample answers:

1. The bottle of soda opened with a <u>fizz</u> and a <u>pop</u>.

2. My stomach <u>gurgled</u> after I drank the milkshake.

3. The snake <u>hissed</u> when it heard us.

4. The gravel <u>crunched</u> beneath the weight of Steven's boots.

Exercise 6

Answers will vary. Sample answers:

1. My room is buried under a mountain of clothes.

2. Mike's head exploded from studying.

3. Ike must have grown twenty feet this year!

4. The car trip took forever.

5. Piper was melting at the beach.

Exercise 7

1. "the shadow I cast as I pedaled raced along my side."
   "The leaves of bird-filled trees stirred a warm breeze . . . . "
   "litter scuttled out of the way."
   "wind tickled the back of my throat."

   > All of these quotes describe an inanimate thing using a human characteristic.

2. Onomatopoeia

3. "Our orange cats looked on from the fence, their tails up like antennas."

4. Sample answer:
   "I opened my mouth as wide as the ocean, and wind tickled the back of my throat."

   > Answers will vary. Does your answer exaggerate for humor or emphasis?

5 Answers will vary. Sample answer:

In this excerpt of "The Bike," Gary Soto uses two kinds of figurative language to create vivid nature imagery, because the scene takes place outside. He mainly uses personification, which makes the world around the character feel very alive and helps the reader imagine all the movement around him as he rides his bike. He also uses a simile, comparing cat tails to antennas. Antennas aren't natural, but they are found outside in neighborhoods, and this simile creates a nice contrast to the breezy, natural descriptions in the rest of the passage.

Exercise 8

Rewritten answers will vary. Yours is correct if it has the same meaning as the phrases underlined in green.

1 Her friends were nervous for the final exam, but Gabby was cool as a cucumber.
   . . . Gabby was calm and unbothered.

2 When her speech received a standing ovation, Akilah knew the election was in the bag.
   . . . Akilah knew she would win the election.

The students were in hot water after the principal found graffiti on her office wall.
   The students were in trouble . . .

3 A good mechanic would never cut corners.
   . . . would never do a job poorly to save time or money.

4 There's no pop quiz—I'm just pulling your leg.
   . . . I'm just joking.

5 To break the ice, Marnie suggested playing two truths and a lie.
   To help start a conversation, Marnie suggested . . .

Exercise 9

1 G

2 F

3 E

4 C

5 B

6 D

7 H

8 A

Exercise 10

Answers will vary. Your answer is correct if:

- The religious allusion is to a story, event, or character from a religious tradition (Christianity, Judaism, Islam, Buddhism, Hinduism, etc.).
- The literary allusion is to a story, event, or character from literature.
- The mythological allusion is to a story, event, or character from any kind of mythology (Greek, Roman, Egyptian, Chinese, Norse, etc.).
- The historical allusion is to an event or figure from world history.

Sample answers:

Mecca is a city where many Muslims make a sacred pilgrimage.

1 **Religious allusion:** New Orleans is a <u>mecca</u> for Jazz musicians.

2 **Literary allusion:** When Emilie's parents forbade her from going on a date, Samira pulled a page out of <u>Romeo's</u> book, and <u>waited under her window.</u>

One of the star-crossed lovers in Shakespeare's Romeo and Juliet.

3 **Mythological allusion:** She ran so quickly, she must have borrowed <u>Hermes's sandals!</u>

Hermes is the Greek messenger god, known for being quick and for wearing sandals with wings.

4 **Historical allusion:** When Matthew snitched on Terrel the class started calling him <u>Benedict Arnold.</u>

A spy during the American Revolution!

CHAPTER 10: WORD CHOICE

Exercise 1

1   Denotation. A hut is a small, modest dwelling. A chalet is a large, extravagant dwelling.

2   Connotation. "Packed" and "crammed" have similar denotations, but "packed" is neutral—it doesn't describe how the bag was packed. "Crammed" gives more information and implies that the bag was stuffed full.

3   Connotation. "Old" and "vintage" have similar denotations, but "old" could imply that the furniture was not in good condition. "Vintage" has a positive connotation and implies that the furniture is cool or has value.

4   Denotation. "Ravenous" means Kiera was still hungry. "Stuffed" means she was uncomfortably full.

5   Connotation. "Chatted" and "gossiped" have similar denotations, but "chatted" is neutral—it doesn't describe the type of chatter. "Gossiped" implies that the team's chatter could be mean or hurtful.

6   Connotation. "Picky" and "selective" have similar denotations, but "picky" implies that Tommy is being difficult, while "selective" implies that he is making thoughtful choices.

7   Denotation. "Comforted" means that the older kids were being kind. "Ridiculed" means they were being mean.

8   Connotation. "Lurched" and "swayed" both describe movement, but "swayed" describes calm movement, while "lurched" implies quick and dangerous movement.

Exercise 2

Sentences will vary. Yours are correct if they provide the proper context for the underlined words. See the sample sentences below.

1 D

has a negative connotation, as if Daniella is being rude or snarky.

I felt sad when Daniella <u>smirked</u> at me from across the room.

I felt happy when Daniella <u>smiled</u> at me from across the room.

has a positive connotation, as if Daniella is being friendly!

2 C

I was <u>brainwashed</u> into thinking apples are better than pears.

Your solid arguments <u>persuaded</u> me that apples are better than pears.

3 G

Joseph <u>babbled</u> on for hours.

Joseph <u>talked</u> for hours.

4 H

The <u>decrepit</u> dog needed a bath.

The <u>old</u> dog needed a bath.

5 F

My parents are so <u>frugal</u>; they won't let us turn on the heat until December!

My parents are so <u>thrifty</u>; they upcycle furniture they find on the curb.

6 A

Those bananas are <u>rotten</u>—throw them away!

Those bananas are <u>overripe</u>—time to make banana bread!

7 B

Her condescending tone made her seem <u>arrogant</u>.
Her calm attitude made her seem <u>confident</u>.

8 E

I <u>snooped</u> through my friend's closet for her necklace.
I <u>searched</u> my friend's closet for her necklace.

Exercise 3

Answers will vary. To check if your answers are correct, ask yourself:

• Is the denotation of my word and the teal word the same?
• Does my explanation show that the word's connotations are different and how the meaning of the sentence changed?

Sample answers:

1 The neighbor was <u>nosy</u>.

Both words mean being interested in learning something. "Nosy" implies the neighbor's curiosity is inappropriate.

2 The <u>clique</u> sat together at lunch.

Both words refer to a group of people, but "clique" implies that the group is snobbish or exclusive.

3 Brian's parents are <u>overbearing</u>.

Both words mean demanding, but "overbearing" implies that the demands are too much, or harmful.

4 Marisa can be very <u>assertive</u>.

Both words mean the person is forceful and confident, but "assertive" implies that Marisa's force is respectful. "Pushy" implies that it might be rude.

5 The music was <u>blaring</u> so loud we didn't hear the fire alarm.

Both words mean the music was playing but "blaring" implies that the music was extremely or uncomfortably loud.

6 Ba rolled down the windows because the car was <u>stifling</u>.

Both words describe the car's hot temperature, but "stifling" adds the meaning that it was unbearably warm.

Answers will vary. Sample answers:

When I found out that my parents had invited the minister's family over for Christmas Eve dinner, I cried. What would Robert think of our shabby Chinese Christmas? What would he think of our noisy Chinese relatives who lacked proper American manners? What terrible disappointment would he feel upon seeing not a roasted turkey and sweet potatoes but Chinese food?

On Christmas Eve I saw that my mother had outdone herself in creating a strange menu. She was pulling black veins out of the backs of fleshy prawns. The kitchen was littered with appalling mounds of raw food: A slimy rock cod with bulging fish eyes that pleaded not to be thrown into a pan of hot oil. Tofu, which looked like stacked wedges of rubbery white sponges. A bowl soaking dried fungus back to life.

1. The narrator feels anxious about the minister's family coming to dinner because she is embarrassed by the ways her cultural traditions differ from those practiced by the American family.

2. Tan chose words that express disgust. The language she uses to describe the foods the narrator's mother prepared makes those foods sound unappealing and unappetizing. (Examples of Tan's word choices will vary, but any of the words and phrases noted in the annotated paragraph are correct.)

3. See the annotated paragraph 1 above for words and phrases with negative denotations and connotations.

4 When I found out that my parents had invited the minister's family over for Christmas Eve dinner, I was overjoyed. What would Robert think of our cozy Chinese Christmas? What would he think of our boisterous Chinese relatives who were unfamiliar with traditional American customs? What an interesting experience it would be for him to eat delicious Chinese food for Christmas, instead of a roasted turkey and sweet potatoes.

5 See the annotated paragraph 2 on the previous page for words and phrases with negative denotations and connotations.

6 On Christmas Eve I saw that my mother had outdone herself in creating a delectable menu. She was skillfully deveining a pile of prawns. The kitchen was overflowing with heaping dishes of raw food: A fresh rock cod with shiny fish eyes ready to be sautéed in a pan of hot oil. Stacks of springy white tofu. A bowl of water rehydrating dried mushrooms.

Exercise 5

Answers will vary.

> Alison, I feel terrible about what happened at school earlier today. I didn't mean to humiliate you in front of everyone. I shouldn't have repeated the story you shared with me in confidence. It was bad enough that you strode out of the bathroom without noticing the toilet paper stuck to your shoe. It was insensitive of me to announce it to the whole class! I'll never forget the expression on your face when the students snickered. I know you are probably furious with me. Can you ever forgive me?

The words you chose are correct if they are synonyms of the words in red!

Exercise 6

Answers will vary.

> The words you chose are correct if they are synonyms of the words in red!

1. Jack sprinted across the finish line and won his first race.

2. Brandi angrily snatched the diary from her snooping sister.

3. "Don't touch the hot stove, Mateo!" the babysitter shrieked.

4. Mae lifted the fragile necklace from the box and carefully tried it on.

5. Scaling up the craggy cliffside was exciting!

6. Mason lugged the heavy buckets of rocks to the garden.

7. After hours of turbulence, the passengers were ecstatic the plane landed safely.

8. When the tiger escaped its cage, the acrobats began to scream!

CHAPTER 11: TONE

Exercise 1

1. E
2. H
3. D

4. A
5. B
6. G

7. C
8. F

Exercise 2

Answers will vary. Sample answers:

1. I will not take no for an answer.

2. If you trade your lunch with me, I'll be your best friend.

3. I guess I will have to go to the party without you.

4. You are one of the nicest people I have ever known.

5. Are you trying to get the whole world's attention with those orange suspenders?

6. I cannot believe you would insult me like that!

7. When we were young, we spent our time outside, playing tag, riding bikes, and climbing trees. Those were the good old days.

8. Tomorrow is Friday the 13th.

Exercise 3

Answers will vary.

2. The nurse gave me a strained smile.   tense
   The nurse gave me a glowing smile.   friendly

3. Corey weaved his way through the crowd.   breezy
   Corey pushed his way through the crowd.   aggressive

4. Georgia was worried about her grades.   concerned
   Georgia was thrilled about her grades.   excited

5. I chuckled as the muddy toddlers waddled through the kitchen.   playful
   I groaned as the muddy toddlers waddled through the kitchen.   defeated

6   Marcus smiled at his younger brother. friendly
    Marcus snarled at his younger brother. threatening

7   The audience howled at the comedian's joke. amusing
    The audience hissed at the comedian's joke. scornful

8   Lincoln snatched the money from his friend's wallet. forceful
    Lincoln slipped the money from his friend's wallet. secretive

Exercise 4

A FEW MILES south of Soledad, the Salinas River drops in close to the hill-side bank and runs deep and green. The water is warm too, for it has slipped twinkling over the yellow sands in the sunlight before reaching the narrow pool. On one side of the river the golden foothill slopes curve up to the strong and rocky Gabilan mountains, but on the valley side the water is lined with trees—willows fresh and green with every spring, carrying in their lower leaf junctures the debris of the winter's flooding; and sycamores with mottled, white, recumbent limbs and branches that arch over the pool. On the sandy bank under the trees the leaves lie deep and so crisp that a lizard makes a great skittering if he runs among them. Rabbits come out of the brush to sit on the sand in the evening, and the damp flats are covered with the night tracks of 'coons, and with the spread pads of dogs from the ranches, and with the split-wedge tracks of deer that come to drink in the dark.

The tone of this passage is calm and peaceful.

Exercise 5

Answers will vary. Sample answers:

1. A few miles south of Soledad, the Salinas River sinks low into the hillside bank and runs bottomless and dark. The water is warm, for reasons no one knows. The water jets from high on the mountain under a cover of trees, without ever seeing the sun.

2. On one side of the river the treacherous foothills twist up the dark and forbidding Gabilan mountains, and on the other side the bank is crowded with shrubs that catch floating debris in their spiny thorns and lined with trees whose scraggly branches jut threateningly over the dark pool.

Exercise 6

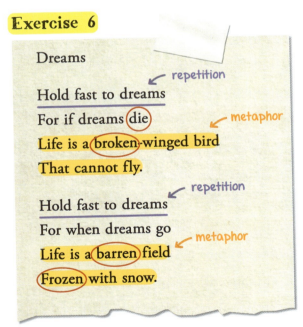

Dreams

Hold fast to dreams ← repetition
For if dreams die
Life is a broken-winged bird ← metaphor
That cannot fly.
Hold fast to dreams ← repetition
For when dreams go
Life is a barren field ← metaphor
Frozen with snow.

1. Honest answers are all correct.

2. The message of the poem is that it is important to have dreams, because dreams give our lives meaning when times are tough.

3 Answers will vary. You might describe the tone as urgent, serious, somber, contemplative, or inspirational.

4 The tone of the poem stays the same. In both stanzas, Hughes uses metaphor to compare a life without dreams to things that are sad or lifeless (a bird with broken wings, a barren frozen field).

5 See the annotated poem on the previous page. Answers will vary. Both metaphors compare a life without dreams to circumstances that would be difficult to live in, which creates a sadness in the reader.

6 See the annotated poem on the previous page. The repeated phrases help convey a serious, somber tone by giving the reader a command, followed by a warning.

CHAPTER 12: TEXTUAL ANALYSIS

Exercise 1

1 E

2 B

3 C

4 G

5 I

6 A

7 D

8 F

9 H

Exercise 2

Answers will vary. You successfully paraphrased the passage if you:
- Restated it in your own words, without using the original language.
- Conveyed the same meaning as the original passage.
- Included important details and left out any details that aren't important.
- Made it shorter and to the point.

Sample answers:

1. Aesop was a writer from ancient Ethiopia who introduced animist tales to Greece. He was brought there as an enslaved person and lived there for the rest of his life. It's not known how, but at some point, he was able to gain his freedom, perhaps due to the popularity of his stories.

2. Glacial ice isn't completely solid; it contains air bubbles that get trapped as snow builds up over time. Air bubbles are captured in the ice as layers of snow pack on top of it. Bubbles in the oldest glacial ice contain air from thousands of years ago.

3. Ghost lights are strange balls of light sometimes visible over bogs and marshes. Some think they are spirits of the dead, trying to trick and confuse people. Scientists think they are probably gas from the bogs catching fire.

4. Mary Shelley was eighteen years old when she wrote the classic novel *Frankenstein*. She came up with the idea while on vacation with her friends. They were stuck inside because of rain and entertained themselves by writing scary stories. Mary might have been inspired to write about a monster that killed its creator because her own mother, feminist writer Mary Wollstonecraft, died giving birth to her.

> This might not be the most relevant detail, but sometimes what's "important" is subjective.

Exercise 3

Margie even wrote about it that night in her diary. On the page headed May 17, 2155 , she wrote, "Today Tommy found a real book !"   implicit evidence

It was a very old book . Margie's grandfather once said that when he was a little boy *his* grandfather told him that there was a time when all stories were printed on paper . . . .

"Gee," said Tommy, "what a waste. When you're through with the book, you just throw it away, I guess. Our television screen must have had a million books on it and it's good for plenty more. I wouldn't throw it away."

"Same with mine," said Margie. She was eleven and hadn't seen as many telebooks as Tommy had.

You probably found more implicit evidence than explicit evidence. That might be because the writer is trying to create a mysterious tone or keep the reader in suspense. He gives some explicit evidence that it takes place in the future, such as the date 2155, but the rest is implied by the way the narrator describes and understands the world around her.

Exercise 4

Answers will vary. Use the following questions to evaluate your response:

- Does your central idea address the prompt?
- Does your evidence support your central idea?
- Do you clearly show how your evidence supports your central idea?
- Do you provide enough context for your central idea and evidence to make sense?
- Does your response paragraph successfully develop your central idea or prove your point?

Sample answer:

In the book *Other Words for Home*, Jude has conflicting views of America. At first, Jude is overwhelmed by the modernity and wealth she sees in the United States. She observes, "In America, it seems like everyone has money," and buys products that make them look wealthy, such as "new shiny sneakers." The more time she spends there, she notices that not everyone in America is wealthy and comfortable. Some people have to beg for help on the street, and wear cracked, worn-out shoes, not "new shiny sneakers." She sees that America is just "like every other place in the world," where some people are well off and others are struggling. It is not the perfect place she was made to think it was.

Exercise 5

Answers will vary. Sample answer:

In May 2023, Joshua Ninmann became the first sixth-grader to win first place in Herricks Middle School's annual spelling bee. Over 100 students in grades 6-8 competed in the spelling bee. Joshua is an honor roll student with a 4.0 GPA, a member of the matheletes club, and serves as sixth grade class treasurer. In 2023, he also won first place at the science fair and published a short story in *Teen Ink*. In June, Joshua will compete in the Scripps National Spelling Bee. If he wins, he will use the prize money to pay for college tuition.

Exercise 6

In *Okay for Now*, the main character Doug Sweiteck <u>has a terrible life</u>! His father is an abusive alcoholic who hits his kids, bullies his wife, and loses one job after another. <u>Doug's father is a miserable man.</u> <u>I think Doug's brothers learned to be abusive from their dad</u> because <u>they are also mean.</u> They follow in their father's footsteps, tormenting Doug by hitting him and bullying him. <u>This is despicable behavior, in my opinion.</u> When Doug receives a signed cap from Joe Pepitone of the New York Yankees, his older brother takes it and passes it around school until it ends up in a rainy gutter. <u>I would be furious if my brother stole something special from me.</u> <u>What's worse</u> is that his father has also lost his job, and so the whole family has to pick up and move to Marysville. Doug is sad he won't be able to attend eighth grade at Camillo Jr. High with his friends. When Doug's family is packing the car to move, his <u>very kind</u> best friend Holling Hoodhood lifts Doug's spirits by giving him Joe Pepitone's signed jacket as a moving away gift. <u>It was such a thoughtful gesture.</u> <u>I would feel so much better if someone did that for me.</u> This shows the theme of the book: good friends can help you cope with the hardships you face.

Answers will vary. Sample answer:

In *Okay for Now*, the main character Doug Sweiteck faces many hardships. His father is an abusive alcoholic who hits his kids, bullies his wife, and loses one job after another. Doug's brothers follow in their dad's footsteps and torment Doug by hitting him and bullying him. When Doug receives a signed cap from Joe Pepitone of the New York Yankees, his older brother takes it and passes it around school until it ends up in a rainy gutter. When Doug's father loses his job, the whole family has to pick up and move to Marysville. Doug is sad he won't be able to attend eighth grade at Camillo Jr. High with his friends. When Doug's family is packing the car to move, his best friend Holling Hoodhood lifts Doug's spirits when he gives him Joe Pepitone's signed jacket as a moving away gift. This shows the theme of the book: good friends can help you cope with the hardships you face.

Exercise 7

Sample answer:

Answers will vary. Use the questions from exercise 4's answer key to check your answers.

Netflix's show *Heartstopper* is a live-action adaptation of the graphic novel series of the same name that follows teenagers Charlie and Nick as they meet and develop crushes on each other. The creators use whimsical elements of animation as metaphors that reveal the character's emotions to the audience.

We see animation for the first time in episode 1, "Meet," when the main character, Charlie, sees Nick for the first time on the first day of school. Two small, animated leaves swirl slowly around Charlie's head, and we hear the sound of rushing wind. This visual metaphor evokes the feeling of possibility and excitement that comes with back to school, autumn, and the possibility of a crush. When Charlie sits next to him and says hi, the animated wind picks up again, this time swirling around both of them, getting faster and faster as the camera focuses on Charlie's smiling face. We might have been able to guess Charlie was feeling hopeful and enchanted by Nick, but the addition of the animation added a whimsical element that makes his feelings clear.

At the end of the episode, Nick defends Charlie from a bully. Charlie sends Nick a thank-you text, and we see him receive it in the car home from school. He reads it and stares out the window with a smile on his face as three small animated seagulls begin flying around his head. We hear ocean waves, and the call of a gull. Once again, these animations evoke a sense of possibility and excitement, signaling to the audience that Nick is feeling the same way as Charlie. Seagulls are also a metaphor for freedom of expression. Charlie is openly gay, but Nick is just discovering these feelings about himself.

The animated elements in *Heartstopper* present the audience with visual metaphors that enhance our understanding of the characters and their emotional arcs, while also adding an air of whimsy and magic that goes along with falling in love for the first time.

UNIT 3
Writing

Exercise 1

1 Second person

2 First person

3 Third person

4 Second person

5 Third person

Exercise 2

Answers will vary. Check if your answers are correct:

- The narrator of the first-person point of view paragraph will use pronouns "I," "me," and "mine."
- The narrator of the second-person point of view paragraph will use pronouns "you" and "yours."
- The narrator of the third-person point of view paragraph will use pronouns "he," "she," "they," "his," "hers," and "theirs."

Sample answers:

First Person

The doorbell rang, but when I looked outside, to my surprise, no one was there. Then I noticed a small, shiny package no larger than a shoe box sitting on the doormat. "What is this?" I muttered to myself. Upon closer inspection, I noticed some scrawled writing on the side: *From your secret admirer.* I wondered if it was some kind of trick. After all, it was late, well after ten p.m., and it was pouring rain! Who would venture all the way here to leave me a gift?

Second Person

The doorbell rings, but when you look outside, to your surprise, no one is there. At your feet, however, is a small, shiny package no larger than a shoe box. "What is this?" you ask yourself. Upon closer inspection, you notice some scrawled writing on the side: *From your secret admirer.* You wonder if this is some type of trick. After all, it is late, well past ten p.m., and it is pouring out. Who would venture all the way here to leave you a gift?

Third Person

The doorbell rang, but when Ali looked outside, to his surprise, no one was there. Then he noticed a small, shiny package no larger than a shoe box sitting on the doormat. "What is this?" he muttered to himself. Upon closer inspection, Ali noticed some scrawled writing on the side: *From your secret admirer.* He wondered if it was some kind of trick. After all, it was late, well past ten p.m., and it was pouring rain! Who would venture all the way here to leave him a gift?

Exercise 3

1. Paris, France (Specifically, the Eiffel Tower!)

2. A sports field during a practice

3. A library in the summertime

4. A campsite at dusk

5. In a spacecraft, orbiting Earth

Exercise 4

Answers will vary. Check if your paragraphs are correct:

- Is there a clear sense of time and place?
- Does your sensory imagery give your reader a picture of where you are? Does it describe things you can taste, touch, smell, hear, see, and feel in your setting?
- Does your paragraph make sense?

Bonus points if you used any figurative language (like metaphors, similes, and personification) or other literary devices (like alliteration, repetition, and rhyme)!

Exercise 5

1. False   Narrative writing can be fiction or nonfiction.

2. True   (But they're not always told in chronological order!)

3. False   Narrative writing tells a story.

4. False   Unreliable narrators can be used for a dramatic effect or to create a surprise twist in the story.

5. False   Narrators can choose to be subjective, sharing their opinions and feelings, or objective, excluding their opinions and feelings.

6. True

7. False   A first-person narrator tells uses the pronoun "I." A third-person narrator uses the pronouns "he," "she," and "they."

8. True

9. False   A narrative needs a conflict to make the story interesting, move the plot along, and help the characters grow.

10. True

Exercise 6

Answers will vary. Sample answer:

TITLE: "The Yellow Wallpaper"

AUTHOR: Charlotte Perkins Gilman

1 It takes place inside a large, isolated house in New England in the late 1800s.

2 The narrator is a woman who is experiencing depression. She is newly married and recently a mother.

3 The narrator uses first-person point of view.

4 "The Yellow Wallpaper" is a series of diary entries written by a new mother who is experiencing postpartum depression. Her husband is also her doctor, and his treatment for her depression is rest. He doesn't let her do things like go outside or write. She keeps a secret diary, where she records sensing something strange and threatening in their house. The room she sleeps in has peeling yellow wallpaper and bars on the windows. As the story progresses, she grows obsessed with the wallpaper and comes to believe there is a woman trapped underneath it. She tries to help the woman escape. By the end of the story, she has a breakdown. She locks herself in the room and begins tearing at the wallpaper. She is convinced that she herself is the woman in the wallpaper. Her husband comes in the room and faints. The story ends with her walking in circles around the room.

5 The conflict is this woman is struggling from postpartum depression, and her suffering is not being taken seriously. She is not given the treatment she needs, and she does not feel respected by the people taking care of her.

6 My favorite character is the narrator, whose name we never learn. She is the most interesting character, and most of the story is told from her point of view. She is thoughtful, passionate, and imaginative. She thinks critically about the experiences of women, and we see firsthand what happens when people, like husbands, don't take women seriously.

7 This character had the most development throughout the story. She starts off depressed and anxious, but hopeful for healing. As the story goes on, she grows paranoid, especially when she isn't getting taken seriously. By the end of the story she experiences a full mental breakdown.

8 The last line of dialogue in the story is "I've got out at last,' said I, 'in spite of you and Jane! And I've pulled off most of the paper, so you can't put me back!'" This is an effective example of dialogue because it reveals the depths of her mental distress, but also her determination to free herself from the physical and metaphorical prison she has been kept in.

9 The story ends with the immediate aftermath of her mental breakdown. Her husband faints as he sees her walking in circles around the room she had just destroyed. The final line of the story implies that she continues walking and just steps over his body on the ground. It did surprise me because it was so open-ended and abrupt. We don't know what happens to any of the characters.

10 "[The wallpaper] sticks horribly and the pattern just enjoys it! All those strangled heads and bulbous eyes and waddling fungus growths just shriek with derision!"

"The color is repellent, almost revolting; a smouldering, unclean yellow, strangely faded by the slow-turning sunlight. It is a dull yet lurid orange in some places, a sickly sulphur tint in others."

". . . a lovely, shaded, winding road, and one that just looks off over the country. A lovely country, too, full of great elms and velvet meadows."

Exercise 7

Answers will vary. Check if your dialogue is correct:
- Does it develop the character's assigned trait?
- Does it advance the plot?
- Does it make sense in the story?

Sample answers:

1 "Mr. Stevens, could I shovel your stoop for you? I love the exercise and could use some more time in the sun!"

2 "It's me! I gave myself a makeover, and I feel more like myself than ever. How was your summer?"

3 "Hey guys, why don't you leave this kid alone. Hi, I'm Rooney. What's your name?"

4 "Ugh, I wish! But I should stay here and study if I want to ace this test. Thank you for the invite though. Maybe next time."

CHAPTER 14: THE WRITING PROCESS

Exercise 1

1 Prewriting

2 Editing

3 Audience

4 Outline

5 Revising

6 Task

7 Publishing

8 Central idea

9 First draft

central idea

They might have tiny brains, but <u>crows are one of the smartest animals on Earth</u>. Scientists say that animals who use tools to complete tasks are intel-

supporting evidence

ligent. <u>Crows use tools to hunt</u>. And they don't just use the tools, they make the tools themselves, and teach each other how. They transform twigs into spears by stripping their leaves and carving hooks into the tip. Then they use these hooked spears to pull bugs and other critters from out of deep hiding

transition words   *supporting evidence*

spots. <u>In addition</u>, <u>they can remember human faces they've seen just one time</u> and will change their behavior towards a person if they recall behavior

transition word

that was dangerous or extra kind. <u>Furthermore</u>, <u>when a human feeds a crow,</u>

<u>or does something kind to take care of it, crows have been known to</u> *supporting*
evidence
<u>bring the person an object as payment</u>. This is called "gifting."
Crows have gifted jewelry, keys, pretty rocks, and even money!

Exercise 3

Answers will vary. Your revised email is correct if you:
- Use polite and formal language to address Mr. Hubbard.
- Ask for what you need, instead of making demands.
- Remove casual language like slang and abbreviations.
- Correct spelling and grammar mistakes.

RE: Interview request regarding new backpack policy

Good morning, Mr. Hubbard,

I am interested in writing an article for our school newspaper about the new backpack policy. Students have recently learned that they can no longer carry backpacks in the hallways or bring them to class. Instead, they must store them in their lockers during the day. Many students are concerned about the change. Do you have any time this week to meet with me so that I may ask a few questions for the story? I am available during my lunch period or any day after school at your convenience.

Thanks for your consideration,
Jason Teller

Exercise 4

1 Revising

2 Prewriting

3 Revising

4 Outlining

5 Publishing

6 Drafting

7 Prewriting

8 Revising

1. The writer's task is most likely to write an argumentative essay.

2. The central idea is that e-readers offer a better reading experience than print books.

3. E-readers are more portable than print books, or, e-readers are more convenient than print books.

4. Any of the details listed under the two supporting ideas is an example of evidence.

5. Answers will vary.
   One additional supporting idea might be that e-readers are more environmentally friendly because they don't use paper.

6. E-readers are more convenient than print books.

7. No, this evidence does not belong in this outline. If the writer was arguing that print books are better than e-readers, this could be a supporting idea.

Exercise 6

Answers will vary. Sample answer:

Introduction: Imagine spending eight hours a day in school, then having three hours of homework.

Central idea: Although there is value to homework, too much can negatively affect students mentally and socially.

Supporting Idea 1: Too much homework can cause stress for students.

    a. Students lead busy lives outside of school.

    b. Sleep deprivation leads to physical and mental health issues.

Supporting Idea 2: Too much homework affects students' ability to engage with their communities.

    a. Students don't have time to spend with friends and family.

    b. Students may have to give up extracurricular activities and hobbies to complete work.

Conclusion: Too much homework impacts students in negative ways. Students can lose joy in learning, become less motivated, and develop a poor attitude toward school. Please support students by advocating for less homework.

Exercise 7

Answers will vary. Sample letter:

To the members of the school board,

Imagine spending a full day in school only to come home to another three hours of homework. School days are long, and students are overwhelmed and exhausted. On behalf of the student body, I ask you to support students by limiting the amount of homework teachers can assign.

Although there is value to homework, too much can negatively affect students mentally and socially. First, too much homework causes stress. Today's students face a lot of pressure. They are asked to get good grades, participate in sports or other extracurricular activities, and do community service. Some students also work part-time jobs after school. It is quite difficult to juggle it all. When teachers assign hours of homework after school, students struggle mentally, and their health is negatively impacted. Often times, students are up all night trying to complete the work, which causes sleep deprivation. And stress causes headaches and stomachaches.

In addition, too much homework also affects students' abilities to engage with their communities. When students spend hours on homework each night and over the weekend, they don't have the time to spend with their friends and family. Isolation leads to depression and self-esteem issues for many teenagers. It is important for teens to have time to relax, unwind, and bond with their peers. Too much homework might lead students to drop interests and hobbies because they don't have time.

In conclusion, too much homework impacts students in negative ways. Students can lose joy in learning, become less motivated, and develop a poor attitude toward school. Please support students by advocating for less homework.

Exercise 8

Believe it or not, Students are not not the only ones who are impacted by to much homework. Parents are also negatively effected. Parents are also busy. Many parents' work full time jobs, and then when they get Home, they have to help their children do homework. Sometimes parents do not now how to help their children sometimes parents do not have the educationally background to help sometimes parents do not speak the language and sometimes their may only be 1 parent at home to help. Which is stressful. And leds to fighting among the parents and child.

Believe it or not, students are not the only ones who are impacted by too much homework. Parents are also negatively affected. Many parents work full-time jobs, and then when they get home, they have to help their children do homework. Sometimes parents do not know how to help their children. Sometimes parents do not have the educational background to help. Sometimes parents do not speak the language, and sometimes there may only be one parent at home to help, which is stressful. All these factors may lead to fighting between the parents and child.

CHAPTER 15: RESEARCH FOR WRITING

Exercise 1

1. This question is too simple; it has one specific answer and doesn't require in-depth research.

2. This question is too simple. It can be answered with "yes" or "no."

3. The question is too broad; an essay exploring this research question would be vague and unfocused.

4. The question is too broad.

5. This question is not researchable.

6. This question is too broad.

Exercise 2

Answers will vary. Sample answers:

1. How has Google changed the ways students learn?

2. How does social media affect the mental health of preteen girls?

3. Can music impact a person's mood?

4. How does climate change affect the sleeping patterns of polar bears?

5. How did Times Square become a tourist attraction for New York City?

6. How did the invention of the iPhone impact communication?

Exercise 3

Answers will vary. Sample answers:

1 What are some negative stereotypes of female characters in video games?

2 Do low grades affect the self-esteem of elementary-aged students?

3 What are the benefits of requiring students to complete community service hours?

4 What are some strategies teens can use to avoid peer pressure?

5 What measures can the United States take to reduce plastic pollution in the ocean?

Exercise 4

Answers will vary. Your answer is correct if:
• Your source helps answer the research question.
• Your source is from a reliable publication.
• Your source is recent and/or relevant.

1 The article "There's a Cell Phone in Your Student's Head," posted by Edutopia on May 6, 2019. Edutopia has been a trustworthy source of information for teachers, educators, and administrators for thirty years. The articles are written and vetted by experts with experience in education.

2 The article "Alternatives to Animals," written by Lisa Learman, and published in *ASBMB Today* in July 2021. *ASBMB Today* is a magazine published by the American Society for Biochemistry and Molecular Biology for its members. A professional magazine is a trustworthy source.

3. The book *Women of the Harlem Renaissance*, edited by Marissa Constantinou, published by HarperCollins in November 2022. This book is a compilation of writings by women of the Harlem Renaissance, with an introduction by a professor of women's history. The work is compiled by an expert, so it can be considered a trustworthy source.

4. The article "How Social Media Is a Toxic Mirror," by Rachel Simmons, published by *Time* magazine on August, 19, 2016. Founded in 1923, *Time* has a reputation for being a credible source.

5. A photograph by Edward S. Curtis, titled *Two Apache Indian women at campfire, cooking pot in front of one*, taken around 1903 and retrieved from the Library of Congress (where it's filed as item 90710166). The Library of Congress is the nation's oldest federal cultural institution, and it serves as the research arm of Congress. It is a credible source.

Exercise 5

Answers will vary. Use these questions to evaluate your answer:
- Does it have a clear central idea, topic sentence, claim, or thesis?
- Does it support that claim with evidence from the research?
- Is the evidence from the article cited in MLA format?

Sample answer:

One of the most anticipated parts of a birthday celebration is the birthday cake. It's a tradition that has been enjoyed for ages. However, after COVID, it is a tradition that should be reconsidered. First, blowing candles on a cake can be unsanitary because bacteria is spread from your mouth to the cake. Dr. S. Patrick Kachur, professor of population and family health at the Columbia University Mailman School of Public Health, explains that blowing out candles "can expel virus particles, just like breathing, talking, singing, shouting, coughing, and sneezing, if the person is infected" (Callahan 2020). Researchers at Clemson University conducted a study in which they assembled a fake cake and put candles on it. They asked eleven subjects to blow on the candles until they were out completely. After conducting this experiment three times over a few days, they discovered, there was 15 times more the amount of bacteria, on average, recovered from the icing compared to the control samples (Sen 2017).

Exercise 6

1 Print book

publication date · *title* · *location* · *publisher*

Thomas, Angie. 2017. *The Hate U Give*. London: Walker Books.

author

2 Online journal article

title · *publication* · *type of source*

Jones, Leo A. "Brain Games." *The Scientific Youth* (online). May 13, 2021.
Accessed June 15, 2022.

author · *date accessed* · *publication date*

3 Newspaper article · *author* · *title*

Schmidt, Sarah. "Companies Fail the Test; Junk Food Marketing Aimed at
Kids Faulted." *The Gazette* [Montreal], March 10, 2010, p. A.11.

publication · *location* · *publication date* · *page*

4 Online article · *author* · *title*

Chen, James. "Industrial Revolution Definition: History, Pros, and Cons."
Investopedia, October 2, 2022, www.investopedia.com/terms/i/industrial-
revolution.asp.

publication · *publication date* · *link*

5 Video · *author* · *title* · *type of source*

Beyoncé. "Beyoncé—Pretty Hurts (Video)." Video posted on YouTube,
April 24, 2014, www.youtube.com/watch?v=LXXQLa-5n5w.

publisher · *publication date* · *link*

Exercise 7

1. The first step is to write a research question.

2. An effective research question is open-ended (not one that can be answered with a yes or no), specific (but not too narrow), interesting, and researchable.

3. You must use credible sources in your research to ensure that your claims are supported by accurate evidence and reliable experts. Your readers will have more confidence in your claims if they see that you have used credible sources. Using sources that aren't credible could result in you including false claims and inaccurate statements in your writing and undermining your point.

4. Credible sources are written by authors who are experts in their field, include relevant and timely research and data, and are published by respected, well-known institutions.

5. Giving credit to your sources makes your writing more credible. It helps your readers access more information for themselves. And it helps you avoid plagiarism.

6. Plagiarism is using another author's exact words or phrases, or their original ideas, without giving them credit. Plagiarism can be avoided by using quotations and citing all your sources.

CHAPTER 16: MEDIA LITERACY

Exercise 1

MEDIA	NOT MEDIA
newspapers	candy wrappers
road signs	butterflies
Public Broadcasting Service (PBS)	Mother Nature
magazines	furniture
TikTok	clothes
Spotify	snow
street graffiti	UNO (card game)
podcasts	
anime	
Netflix	
email	
graphic novels	
YouTube	
commercials	
cave drawings	
birthday card	
slogan	

Exercise 2

Answers will vary.

1. WSJ Graphics

2. It is a social media post that includes a link to a news article and a caption. The link includes a headline and an image. It also includes information around the social media post itself—the handle and profile picture of the account that posted it, as well as the time and date it was posted, and the number of views it received.

3. Sensational language like "record low" and "lowest levels" are used to attract the reader's attention. These words create a sense of urgency and novelty that will attract the reader's attention. The image of an empty classroom underscores that urgency, connecting the idea of low test scores with empty classrooms.

4. Eighth-grade history and civics test scores are low, setting a record.

5. The post is missing specific data that shows details of past test scores.

6. Teachers, students, and parents/caregivers

7. That of eighth-grade students

Exercise 3

Answers will vary. Sample answers:

1 This is a print advertisement for a brand of cereal. It shows someone eating cereal at night when they play video games. It includes a slogan: "Not just for breakfast"!

2 You cannot tell where the media comes from. It is likely that the company who makes the cereal paid for the advertisement.

3 This media is trying to influence the viewer to buy this brand of cereal. It is also trying to encourage the reader to see cereal as something that can be eaten as a snack, or at times other than breakfast. It seems to be made for teenagers or young adults. Lots of information is missing including how much the cereal costs and nutrition information.

Exercise 4

1 B

2 C

3 A

4 A

5 A

6 C

7 A

Exercise 5

1 No

2 No

3 Yes

4 No

5 No

6 Yes

7 No

8 Answers may vary. The article lacks evidence and details. It gives no information about its sources, like author or date. The claim is outrageous. The headline is sensationalized. These are all valid reasons to distrust this piece of media.

Exercise 6

Answers may vary.

1 The author is an eighth-grader who has taken standardized tests for many years.

2 The author wants to communicate that they don't feel standardized tests are a fair measurement of what a student knows. They want to point out the issues they experienced so things can be improved.

3 The message does not talk about the benefits of standardized tests or any positives that the student experienced. It also does not offer any alternatives or solutions.

4 Some people might interpret this message as true and important, if they have experienced something similar or have watched their students experience it. Others might interpret this message as complaining or biased because it doesn't talk about the benefits.

5 Students who are in a similar situation might benefit from this message because they will feel seen and validated. People who create the tests, or work in the education department might benefit if they take it as serious feedback and make changes that help students in this position.

Exercise 7

1 C

2 C

3 B

4 C

5 B

6 C

7 A

8 C

9 A

Exercise 8

1 Yes

2 Yes

3 No

4 Yes

5 No

6 Yes

7 Yes

8 No

9 No

10 Yes

CHAPTER 17: EXPOSITORY WRITING

Exercise 1

1. Explanatory writing. The passage is laying out the steps to making an omelet, or explaining how to make an omelet.

2. Informative writing. The passage is providing information about pocket mice.

3. Both. The passage is informing readers of two habits they can adopt to keep their skin healthy and explaining why those habits are effective.

4. Explanatory writing. The passage is explaining how to do an anxiety-reducing exercise.

5. Informative writing. The passage is informing the reader about a topic.

Exercise 2

1. Classification

2. Example

3. Comparison and contrast

4. Description

5. Classification

6. Definition

7. Cause and effect

8. Narration

9. Example

10. Process analysis

Exercise 3

1. The species of fish humans commonly eat could go extinct within fifty years, and this loss will create a domino effect that has a negative impact on other species and the environment.

2. Kurlansky explains that all species depend on other species. The loss of one species will cause the species who rely on them for food to be in danger and perhaps go extinct themselves.

3) He offers the example of a food chain starting with the fish, which are eaten by seabirds, who provide food to insects such as beetles and lizards.

4) The intended audience is young people who are still in school and who, armed with knowledge, can take action to save the environment. Kurlansky references "people who are in school today" specifically and speaks directly to the reader when he says, "You have more opportunities and more responsibilities than any other generation in history."

5) The primary mode of development is cause and effect: The Industrial Revolution changed the relationship between people and nature. It illustrates how the current generation needs to take action to reverse the destruction of the environment.

6) Kurlansky references Darwin's work because Darwin is generally recognized as a credible source, and in his book, he explained that all species prey on and kill other species to survive. We, along with many other species, eat fish and need fish to survive.

7) Classification; this text lists the categories of plant and animal identification.

8) Comparison; Kurlansky compares codfish to humans.

9) Informative

Exercise 4

Answers will vary. Sample answer:

The writer's central idea is that ChatGPT will change the way people communicate. The writer begins with a short anecdote. This narration reveals the reason why ChatGPT is necessary: Writing can be challenging. Humans are always looking for inventions to make their lives easier. The writer also continues developing by not only providing a definition of ChatGPT for readers who may not be familiar with this new technology but also several impressive examples of what ChatGPT can do. From writing an email to recommending a movie, ChatGPT has the capacity to help us communicate more efficiently.

The writer also compares and contrasts older technology with improved technology. The writer also shows a possible effect of using the technology: Workers may be out of jobs!

Exercise 5

Answers will vary. Sample answer:

Topic: The automobile

MODE OF DEVELOPMENT	EXAMPLE
Definition	An automobile is usually a four-wheeled automotive vehicle designed for passenger transportation.
Classification	The Benz Patent Motor Car is considered to be the world's first automobile. Today there are many makes and models: convertibles, sedans, sports cars, coupes, and minivans, to name a few.
Comparison and contrast	The early models of the automobile were very different from the cars of today. They differ in design, components, and capabilities.
Cause and effect	The invention of the automobile gave people more personal freedom and access to jobs and services.
Narration	When my sister got her driver's license, she was able to start driving us to school in our grandma's car. My mom's mornings became more relaxed, and she can pick up earlier shifts at work sometimes. Using another car has helped my family's mornings get a lot easier!
Process analysis	In order to drive a car safely, you need to position yourself comfortably in the driver's seat. Next, fasten your seatbelt and check your rear and side mirrors to make sure you can see effectively. Adjust the mirrors if you can't see effectively.
Description	The first car was a compact two-seater vehicle built on a tubular steel frame with three wire-spoked wheels.
Example	The original car was designed differently from the modern car. For example, the original models did not have windshields or doors.

Exercise 6

Answers will vary. Does your paragraph:
- Have a clear central idea?
- Develop your topic using at least two modes of development?
- Make sense?

Sample answer:

introduction with a hook

Each day, people drive their cars to work and school. They drive their cars to run errands, and they drive their cars to go on trips and take vacations. They probably don't realize what a privilege it is to own a car. Life wasn't always this easy or convenient. Before the invention *cause and effect* of the car, people didn't have as much freedom and mobility. They had limited access to supplies and goods, and they had to find work close to where they lived. Now we have all kinds of cars, from pickup trucks and minivans to electric hatchbacks! Lives changed with the arrival of *classification* the Benz Patent Motor Car in 1886. According to the article "Automobile History" on History.com, it is hard to give credit for the automobile to *cited source* just one single person since many people contributed to its making; however, many historians give credit to Nicolas-Joseph Cugnot. Although there may be disagreement regarding its true inventor, all can agree, the car was a game changer, revolutionizing the modern world. *central idea*

Exercise 7

1 I
2 G
3 E
4 B

5 H
6 F
7 C
8 J

9 A
10 D

Exercise 1

1 Persuasive

2 Argumentative

3 Argumentative

4 Persuasive

5 Argumentative

6 Persuasive

7 Argumentative

8 Persuasive

Exercise 2

1 Reason

2 Counterclaim

3 Introduction

4 Reason

5 Evidence

6 Concession

7 Claim

8 Conclusion

9 Evidence

10 Rebuttal

Exercise 3

1 Their parents

2 That the family's vacation should be a cross-country road trip, instead of a cruise.

3 They would be able to spend more time together as a family.

4 Pathos. They appeal to their parents' emotions by reminding them that they won't be able to have this kind of quality time together for much longer.

5 No.

6 Answers will vary.

Exercise 4

1. There are many valuable benefits for students who continue reading during the summer.

2. Summer reading programs can prevent summer learning loss and enhance student achievement.

3. The writer uses facts about education research and quotes from a report titled "Summer Learning Loss: What Is It and What Can Be Done About It?"

4. In the third paragraph, the writer addresses the counterclaim that summer reading is not a pleasure but another task to be completed.

5. The writer responds to the counterclaim with a concession, acknowledging that the complaint is true to some extent.

Exercise 5

1. Logos

2. Ethos

3. Logos

4. Pathos

5. Ethos

6. Pathos

Exercise 6

1. Thunberg claims world leaders are not doing enough to curb climate change. Their inaction will hurt future generations.

2. Thunberg demonstrates that her perspective is valuable and relevant by showing that she is well educated on the topics and by positioning herself as one of the people who will inherit the problems her audience has failed to address.

3. She shows how the "50% chance of staying below 1.5 degrees Celsius" is not an acceptable risk by outlining the reasons that it is clear it won't be possible to do. This is a logical argument, backed by data and sound reason.

4 "You have stolen my dreams and my childhood with your empty words and yet I'm one of the lucky ones. People are suffering. People are dying. Entire ecosystems are collapsing. We are in the beginning of a mass extinction, and all you can talk about is money and fairy tales of eternal economic growth. How dare you!" Thunberg's appeal to pathos here is effective because her use of strong language directly asks the audience to think about their role in climate change and potentially evokes feelings of desperation, shame, and guilt.

5 Thunberg's speech is an example of persuasive writing. In addition to facts, it uses passionate, emotional language that evokes feelings of urgency and remorse. Her purpose is to persuade politicians to adopt her perspective and act accordingly. In addition, she presents her side of the issue without addressing or introducing counterclaims.

Exercise 7

Answers will vary. Check if your email meets the criteria:

• Does your email state the claim clearly?
• Does it include all three appeals (logos, ethos, and pathos) at least once?
• Do appeals to pathos use language, anecdotes, or examples that will evoke emotions in your teacher?
• Do appeals to ethos demonstrate that you are trustworthy and of good character?
• Do appeals to logos provide information or logical supports to your claim?

Sample answer:

Dear Mrs. Scardina,

As the marking period comes to an end, I see that my current average in your English class is an 89%. I am writing to ask you if you would consider bumping up my average just one percentage point, to 90%. ← claim
While a B+ is certainly not a poor grade, I was hoping to earn an A. With an A, my grade point average will rise to 3.8, which is the GPA required ← logos

logos for eligibility for the National Jr. Honor Society. Ever since I started middle school, it has been my goal to become a member of the school's chapter. **pathos** Both of my older siblings were inducted, and I don't want to be the only one in my family to miss out on this opportunity. It would disappoint my parents and devastate me. **ethos** The first two quarters I received As, and you know that I work hard, submit all my homework, and love to participate. I always come to class on time, and I also come to after-school help class each week to get guidance and feedback on all of my work. Please let me know if there is any extra credit I can do before the quarter ends to bring up my grade up one percentage point. It would mean everything to me. **pathos**

Sincerely,

Your student

Ethos: You show that you are hardworking, motivated, and always on time. In addition, your email is respectful in tone. This speaks to your trustworthiness and good character.

Logos: You note that you received As in the first two quarters of the school year, and you emphasize that your current GPA is only one percentage point from an A. In addition, you state the GPA needed for the National Jr. Honor Society. These facts logically demonstrate that your request is reasonable.

Pathos: You appeal to Mrs. Scardina's sympathy using a personal anecdote, explaining that without this extra point, you will be the only one in your family not to be inducted into the honor society. This personal insight may help your teacher empathize with your situation.

Exercise 8

Brainstorms will vary.

Exercise 9

Outlines will vary. Sample outline:

I. Introduction

    a. Context: Explain the new football bills that are being proposed.

    b. Claim: These bills should be passed because football is dangerous for young players, whose bodies and brains are still developing.

II. Reason 1: Reoccurring head hits can cause serious brain injury.

    a. Evidence: Head hits cause brain diseases (study).

    b. Evidence: Helmets do not adequately protect players from head hits (study).

III. Reason 2: Children's brains are still developing, so they are at greater risk than teens and adults.

    a. Evidence: Quote from doctor saying children's brains are less capable of repairing themselves.

    b. Evidence: Quote saying young kids have weaker neck muscles, so helmets are less effective.

IV. Counterclaim: There is not enough proof that football is dangerous to kids to warrant a law that bans it.

    a. Concession: None! ← That's ok! You don't have to concede if it doesn't make sense to do so.

    b. Rebuttal: Health experts set age minimums for all sorts of activities, like drinking, smoking, and driving, and the science is never purely black and white (quote from expert).

V. Conclusion

  a. Summary of the argument

  b. Takeaway: There are fun and safe alternatives, like flag football!

Exercise 10

Essays will vary. Sample essay:

introduction

context

With more research coming to light over the years about football injuries, many people, including politicians, are reconsidering youth football. New York and California are two states reintroducing bills that would ban tackle football for children under 12 years old. These bills should be passed because football is dangerous for players whose bodies and brains are still developing. *claim*

reason 1 One reason these bills should be passed is because reoccurring hits to the head can cause serious brain injury. A current study in the journal *Brain* "showed evidence of the degenerative brain disease, chronic traumatic enceph-alopathy, or C.T.E., in teenage athletes who sustained head impact injuries" (Belson). While efforts have been made to protect players by requiring them to wear helmets, Dr. Feeley of University of California at San Francisco does not believe helmets are enough to protect the brain from impact. Feeley claims that a helmet "doesn't prevent a concussion" (Johns). *evidence*

reason 2 Another reason these bills should be passed is that football is especially dangerous to children because their brains are still developing. Doctors have discovered that "head hits absorbed by young players are more damaging *evidence* because their brains are not fully developed, and are less capable of fully repairing themselves" (Belson). Doctors also note that "younger players also have weaker neck muscles, and therefore are less capable of bracing for impact and supporting the weight of a football helmet" (Belson).

Some critics of the bill claim that there is not enough proof that *counterclaim* "youth football can lead to Chronic traumatic encephalopathy, a brain condition thought to be linked to repeated head injuries and blows to the head" (Chasmar). However, there are already many laws that restrict youth from *rebuttal* participating in risky behaviors. Dr. Robert Cantu, the cofounder and *evidence* medical director of the Concussion Legacy Foundation, explains, "Some of my colleagues quibble that the science has not determined which age is the right age, but they don't seem to realize that health experts set age minimums for all sorts of activities like drinking, smoking and driving, and the science is never purely black and white" (Belson).

summary of argument A bill banning children from playing football is necessary to protect them. And luckily, there are safer alternatives to football that children under 12 can participate in, like flag football, and they are just as fun.

conclusion

takeaway

416

Everything You Need to Ace English Language Arts is right here!

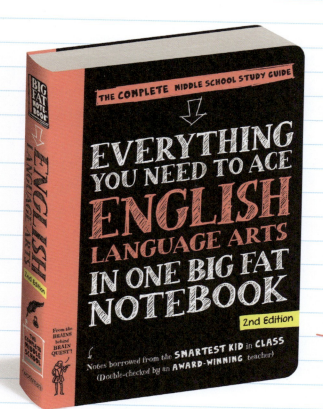

This **Big Fat Notebook** makes all the stuff you need to know sink in with key concepts reinforced through **mnemonic devices, easy-to-understand definitions, doodles**, and more!

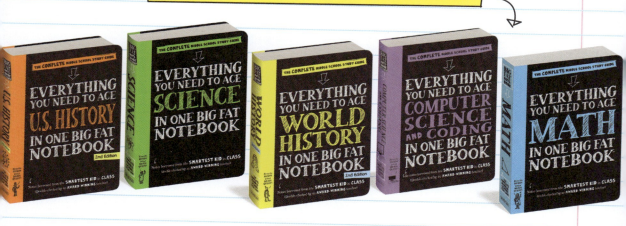

workman